Willie Covan
Loved to Dance!

Dedications

For all who follow their
dreams, great and small—
especially for my husband, Ed.
—S.S.

To Nanette,
who never let anything
stop her many talents!
—C.V.W. & Y.H.H.

FOR INFORMATION CONTACT:
MONDO Publishing
980 Avenue of the Americas
New York, NY 10018
Visit our web site at http://www.mondopub.com

Printed in China

04 05 06 07 08 09 10 HC 9 8 7 6 5 4 3 2 1
04 05 06 07 08 09 10 PB 9 8 7 6 5 4 3 2 1

ISBN 1-59034-445-6 (hardcover)   ISBN 1-59034-580-0 (pbk.)

COVER AND BOOK DESIGN BY Michelle Farinella

Library of Congress Cataloging in Publication Data
Shahan, Sherry
Willie Covan loved to dance / by Sherry Shahan ; illustrated by
Cornelius Van Wright and Ying-Hwa Hu p. cm.
ISBN 1-59034-445-6 – ISBN 1-59034-580-0 (pbk)
1. Covan, Willie, 1897-1988—Juvenile literature. 2. Dancers—United
States—Biography—Juvenile literature. [1. Covan, Willie, 1897-1988.
2. Dancers. 3. Tap dancers. 4. African Americans – Biography .]
I. Van Wright, Cornelius, ill. II. Hu, Ying-Hwa, ill. III. Title.
GVI785.C67S53 2004
792.7'8'092-dc21   2003050984

Willie Covan Loved to Dance!

BY SHERRY SHAHAN

ILLUSTRATED BY Cornelius Van Wright and Ying-Hwa Hu

Clickety-clack.
Clickety-clack
Clickety-
clack.

At 5:30 A.M. the city

was silent except for the sound of electric

streetcars whizzing on by.

Clickety-clack.

Clickety-clack.

Clickety-clack.

Young *Willie Covan* stood on a curb listening, listening.

He pounded out time, shaking his feet—lively toe tapping to a streetcar beat.

It was Chicago, Illinois, 1902, and the beginning of the twentieth century. It was also the beginning of Willie's dream—to see his name in lights at The Palace Theatre. That's how you knew you had made it as a performer, playing THE PALACE.

Willie was black. But Willie wasn't about to let prejudice hold him back. Day after day, he practiced tapping up and down the city streets.

On rooftops,
    in soda shops.
On empty stages,
    in alleyways.

Clickety-clack!
    Clickety-clack!

Willie Covan never studied rhythm at any dance studio. The streets of Chicago were his teachers.

The **pitter-patter**, **clatter** of new buildings going up and old ones coming down. The **rasp and boom** of the trains overhead. The feel of concrete and steel. The city's heartbeat **pulsed** through Willie's feet, teaching him what he needed to know about swinging rhythm.

Snakey hips.

Jive splits.

Mule kicks.

pitter-patter
rhythm
rasp and boom
pitter-patter

Willie Covan

just loved to dance! By his sixth birthday,

he was dancing in minstrel shows,

his **tapping** toes pounding out

music, lively as fingers on a keyboard.

The crowds loved him. Some even hugged him.

"Dance, Willie, dance!"

In those days, performers rubbed burnt cork on their faces to play black folks:

snake charmers,

       song-and-dancers,

joke-and-laugh men,

     juggling acts, acrobats,

      lots of folly,

        and sisters Dolly.

During that time, black singers and dancers

weren't allowed in shows with white performers.

So Willie and the other black children had

to cork up, too, so no one would

know they were black.

IMAGINE THAT!

At the show one fine day,

a white singer named Cosie Smith caught Willie's act.

She so admired his lightning-fast feet that she asked him

to go on tour with her out West. She knew that a dancer

like Willie would guarantee that her routine had a socko

finish. And Willie knew working in a traveling minstrel

show might be his chance to break into the big time,

THE PALACE THEATRE!

The West Coast lay plains and mountain ranges away

from Chicago—a whole wide world away from home.

Willie was afraid to ask his parents. What if they said no?

He fretted and fussed until they said,

"You have our blessing to go with the show."

The next week, Willie, his younger brother, Dewey, and four other singers and dancers rode the rails west. The young performers traveled in coach cars divided into two identical sections—one for white passengers, one for blacks. A flip-over sign, mounted on the bulkhead, divided the white passengers from the black passengers. One side of that sign read WHITES ONLY, the other side COLOREDS.

Through dirty windows, Willie took in open stretches of land and the blur of prairie towns. All the time he was listening to the choo-chug-choo of steel wheels rolling on down the track—his lively feet doodling and noodling to the heel-toe-heel-toe tempo.

choo-chug-choo
choo-chug-choo

In Roundup, Montana,

Willie and his friends played to a bunch of

rowdy cowpunchers in rawhide chaps

who spurred horses into a dance hall.

These guys had never seen a black person

before. But, as Willie said, "They didn't

care nuthin' about no prejudice."

They just whooped it up.

"Come on, dance!"

the cowpunchers yelled.

"Show us what you got!"

Willie and the other dancers hoofed it across the rough-hewn plank floor. They laid down some fancy iron—sliding their feet to a low-down beat, a real barn burner. *Shim, sham, shimmy!*

Tunes of the times danced in the smoky saloon light, shaking the fancy chandeliers. "Let Me Call You Sweetheart," "Polly Wolly Do Da Day," and "Goody Goody Gumdrops."

OH, GOODY, GOODY GUMDROPS

MY HEART IS DOING FLIP-FLOPS

GEE, WHAT LOVE CAN DO!

I'M GONNA SHOUT IT FROM THE ROOFTOPS:

GOODY, GOODY GUMDROPS!

Shim, sham, shimmy!
Shim, sham, shimmy!
Shim, sham, shimmy!

13

One night, after the act, a teenaged kid dashed backstage to share peanuts and sweet snacks with the dancers. "What ya doin' after the show?" he asked them.

"Nuthin'," Willie said.

"You wanna make some money?" he asked.

Well, who didn't?

Willie, Dewey, and their friends piled into a Model T. With tires straining under the weight of so many passengers, the car jostled over chuckholes in the unpaved road. Dust thick enough to chew and spit out spilled in through the windows.

Willie hung on while the car lurched over back-breaker bumps, his feet stirring up a new beat on the wooden floorboards. Bumpity-bump, *jostle-and-jump*. The tires treading heavy—the tailpipes scraping dirt.

Miles and miles of ruts later, they saw lights winking at them in the distance—a real Wild West saloon.

Willie sauntered in and moseyed
up to the bar. "We're here to sing and dance,"
he told the bartender.

Gunslinging cowboys gathered around
while Willie and his friends sang "Sweet Adeline."

SWEET ADELINE

MY ADELINE,

AT NIGHT, DEAR HEART,

FOR YOU I PINE;

IN ALL MY DREAMS,

YOUR FAIR FACE BEAMS.

YOU'RE THE FLOWER OF MY HEART,

SWEET ADELINE.

Man, they danced like crazy!

Flip-flop.
Twist-drop
Spin to a split.

The cowboys went crazy, too, tossing coins on the floor. The dancers snatched up the money and stuffed it in their pockets, never missing a beat. The cowboys kept whooping and hollering— they got so riled up they fired off their guns.

Willie just kept picking up coins. **"We were having a high time!"** he said.

Outside, the kid who'd driven them to the saloon asked if they'd made any money. "Oh, yeah! We made a bundle!" Willie said with sagging britches. "Our pockets are full of pennies. We probably made five or ten dollars—each!"

Plink, plunk, clink!

Willie turned his pockets inside out and started counting. That's when he discovered the cowboys hadn't been throwing pennies. They had been throwing gold coins. The dancers had earned eleven hundred dollars in one night!

When Cosie Smith's tour ended, Willie and his brother rode the rails back to Chicago.

Willie saw a billboard advertising a dancing contest that invited both blacks and whites to compete.

In the theater on the day of the contest, each dancer got a number. Willie drew number eight.

The orchestra tuned up, and the emcee called out, "Number one!"

Under the stage, more than a half dozen Execution Judges tuned their ears to the contestant's timing and rhythm.

Under the stage listening to footfalls? Oh, man!

The Time Judges took notes in the wings, and the Style Judges huddled down in the orchestra pit.

There were judges everywhere . . . everywhere except in the audience.

The first boy peeled off a Time Step: stomp-hop-shuffle-step-flap-step-stomp.

Willie watched in the wings with a case of stage fright. "Number two!"

This dancer plunged into a Time Step, too. In fact, all the dancers did the same stomp-hop-shuffle-step.

Finally it happened. "Number eight!"

Willie's jitters ran all the way down to his toes.

"Number eight!" the emcee repeated.

You done lost already shakin' like this! Willie thought. Willie pushed down his fear

and laced his shoes up tight. Then he stormed the stage and slammed straight into Around the World,

never touching the floor with his hands. Slam! Bam! Spin!

Willie tapped 'til his brand-new hundred-dollar suit unraveled.

"It was worth it," he said. No one had ever done that step without using his hands before.

Willie's whole family was there to see him win that contest. Backstage, they hoisted him onto their shoulders and

carried him through the city streets all the way home. Everyone in town was saying, "Man, that little

Covan boy is something else!"

The contest winnings financed Willie's trip to New York City where he played the T.O.B.A. circuit theaters—black entertainers performing for black audiences. Tap dancing had been around for more than half a century, but it was now taking off at a record clip and soon to be an established American art form—a truly American art form.

During this time, Willie tapped with a lot of dancers, including a soft-shoe hoofer named Leonard Ruffin. They called their act "Every Move a Picture."

This duo was the first with black dancers to perform a piece called the Class Act in the top circuit theaters.

This precision routine required executing identical steps in the most sophisticated style. Their high-style steps were in sweet unison, all laced with a smooth-moving grace. Around 1917, in the northern cities, the color barrier began to crumble—Covan and Ruffin were hired to dance in white vaudeville theaters.

THE BROADHURST THEATRE   THE MAJESTIC   PALAIS D'OR

Willie's toe-tapping feet were one step closer to his big dream, playing THE PALACE THEATRE.

Then in 1926, more than twenty years after Willie first shuffled his feet to a streetcar beat, Covan and Ruffin were

asked to dance in a theater on Broadway at 47th Street in New York City . . . the greatest vaudeville

theater in the world, THE PALACE!

pick pick pick

At rehearsal on the day of their debut, a piano player named Eubie Blake hunkered in the corner, plinking out a song one note

at a time. Willie kept listening to the tune while he and Ruffin worked on their routine: t a p , t a p , t a p , t a p .

That keyboard tickler winked at Willie. "Hey, man, why don't you use this song in your act tonight?"

Something about the sweet beat tickled Willie's feet, so he decided to change the last routine in their act to

fit the song. Everyone thought he was crazy!

tap tap tap

pick pick pick

That night fast shiny automobiles pulled up in front of the theater

to let out folks as swanky as the velvet seats inside. There were flappers with

bobbed hair and gangsters with gats . . . elegant women in gowns and

furs and gentlemen in flashy tuxedos with silk scarves and high top hats.

As the orchestra played "Sweet Georgia Brown,"

the sizzling sound of taps spilled over the footlights and flooded the

audience, slick and quick as a new pair of patent leather shoes.

No dancers had ever tapped in such perfect time to a song.

WHO STOPS THE TRAFFIC DOWN AT 5TH AND MAIN?

SWEET GEORGIA, GEORGIA BROWN

WHO DRIVES ALL THE YOUNG LADS INSANE?

SWEET GEORGIA, GEORGIA BROWN

I AIN'T GONNA LEAVE THIS TOWN

LONG AS GEORGIA'S HANGIN' AROUND

GEORGIA CLAIMED HER, GEORGIA NAMED HER

SWEET GEORGIA BROWN.

26

Downtown hipsters clapped. "That's where it's at!" Uptown hepcats knee-slapped. **"Give us more!"**

Everyone in the theater yelled, "Encore! Encore!"

"Sweet Georgia Brown," became an overnight success—folks left that theater humming Eubie's arrangement. Covan and Ruffin were hotter than a pot of spicy gumbo. No act could follow them.

Willie beamed in the limelight. **"We can keep time spinnin' on a dime!"**

The manager tried to rearrange the bill, but no matter where he put Covan and Ruffin, they stopped the show. For three days—five shows a day—any act that followed the dancing duo was booed off stage.

Now the manager could've solved the problem by putting Covan and Ruffin in the spot next to last. But that was the star spot, the most important place on the bill, and back then a colored act couldn't have top billing at theaters like THE PALACE.

Finally, the manager found a solution. "You're fired!"

A hotshot theater called THE HIPPODROME picked them up right quick. But after three days of stopping the show at the 'drome, they were fired at that theater, too.

But Willie Covan loved to dance. No prejudice would hold him back! Not now, not ever. Man, he was one hot hoofer.

Dance, Willie, dance!

Tap! Tap!

Clickety-clack!

The End

Author's Note

Born on March 4, 1897, in Atlanta, Georgia, *Willie Covan* spent 60 years in show business. He's credited with creating classic tap steps, such as the Rhythm Waltz Clog, and is also known for his Soft Shoe and Buck and Wing. In more than one dance contest, Willie ruined brand-new suits by doing Around the World—with no hands.

Willie traveled the globe with the legendary quartet The Four Covans—Willie, his wife Florence, brother Dewey, and Carita Harbert—thrilling audiences in towns large and small, truly an international sensation.

In the 1930s, when movie musicals became the rage, Willie moved to Hollywood and began working with legendary screen stars, including Shirley Temple, Mickey Rooney, Mae West, and Ann Miller. Eleanor Powell, a top screen tap dancer, insisted Willie be named head dance instructor at MGM Studios, where he became the resident choreographer.

Willie Covan died in Los Angeles, California, on May 7, 1989, but his style of dance lives on. You can still see Willie's tap steps in dance studios, on theater stages, in movies, and probably in more than a few alleyways.

Glossary

AROUND THE WORLD: A popular movement of the 1920s in which the dancer sets his hands on the floor, squats down in an open position using one foot to balance, then swings the free leg under the other leg and hands—lifting the leg and hands and dropping them as the leg swings around.

BARN BURNER: This expression describes a dance so "hot" it could nearly burn down a barn.

BECAME THE RAGE: A style of dance that suddenly becomes popular. The term may also refer to other forms of art, such as painting, music, and poetry.

BUCK AND WING: An American clog dance marked by wing-like steps danced mostly on the balls of the feet.

CHUCKHOLE: A hole or pit in an unpaved road; also called a "pothole."

CLASS ACT: A style of dance performed by a duo or trio in which the dancers tap their steps in unison with one another.

EXECUTION JUDGES: Execution Judges listened to the rhythm and timing of dancers' "taps" during dance contests. Often, these judges were positioned under the stage.

FANCY IRON: The expression describes a difficult tap step. The word "iron" refers to the metal taps on the bottom of tap shoes.

FLAPPERS: These young women of the 1920s were known for their stylish dress and unconventional way of life.

THE FOUR COVANS: One of the first black Class Acts, which used precision to execute steps together with high style and grace. A top act from 1920–1930, they headlined on Broadway, in vaudeville, and in movies. The Four Covans included Willie's wife, Florence, his brother, Dewey, and Carita Harbert.

GAT: An old-time term for a pistol.

HEPCAT: A person who is interested in swing and jazz music.

HIPSTER: A person who follows the latest fads and trends.

HOOFER: Another word to describe a person who dances.

KEYBOARD TICKLER: A slang term for a person who plays the piano.

MINSTREL SHOWS: The first public performance of a minstrel show was given in 1843 by the Virginia Minstrels. These white performers used burnt cork to blacken their faces (called "blackface") and wore gaudy costumes. Shiny white makeup around the eyes and mouth gave the impression of bulging eyes and large lips. This caricature of black men was a grotesque stereotype, which stayed in the minds of white American audiences for many decades.

RECORD CLIP: This expression describes an event that happens very rapidly.

RODE THE RAILS: An old-fashioned saying that means traveling by train.

SOFT SHOE: A dance performed in slow time, originally danced with sand sprinkled on the floor or without metal taps.

STOPPIN' THE SHOW: This expression describes an act so popular with theater audiences that the applause stopped the show. Performers attempting to follow such an act were booed off stage.

T.O.B.A. (Theatre Owners Book Association): Before the First World War, a black comedian from Washington, D.C., named Sherman Dudley, began leasing and purchasing theaters. He also contacted theater owners in the South and Southwest. At its peak the network connected over 300 theaters, forming a black vaudeville circuit: black entertainers performing in black theaters. The musical comedy productions included comedy skits, chorus numbers, and lots of tap dancing.

TIME STEP: One of the most common tap steps danced at the beginning of a routine. Originally used to establish the tempo of a routine for the musicians since rehearsals were rarely held in small-time vaudeville theaters.

VAUDEVILLE: American vaudeville was a type of onstage entertainment that was made up of unrelated songs, dances, acrobatic feats, magic acts, and funny skits. From its beginnings in barrooms in the late 1800s, vaudeville was the main attraction in hundreds of theaters throughout the United States until 1932, when its greatest venue, The Palace Theatre in New York, became a movie theater.

WALTZ CLOG: Originally performed in clog shoes with wooden soles, this step beats out a rhythm in 3/4 time.

Bibliography

Amending Interstate Commerce Act (Segregation of Passengers), Hearings before the Committee on Interstate and Foreign Commerce, House of Representatives, 83rd Congress, 2nd Session, May 12–14, 1954.

Ames, Jerry and Siegelman, Jim. *The Book of Tap, Recovering America's Long-Lost Dance.* New York: David McKay, 1977.

Frank, Rusty E., ed. *Tap! The Greatest Tap Dance Stars and Their Stories, 1900-1955.* New York: Da Capo Press, 1994.

Vaudeville Times, American Museum of Vaudeville, Inc. Volume II, Issue 1, 1999.

www.goldcoast-railroad.org/jimcrow.htm

Retinal Dialyses **Plate 22**

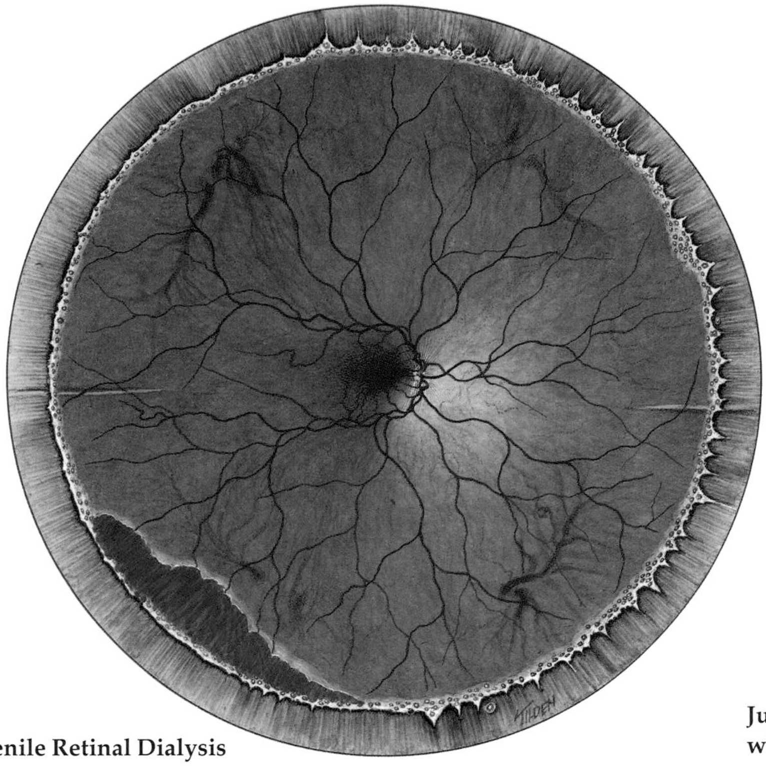

Juvenile Retinal Dialysis

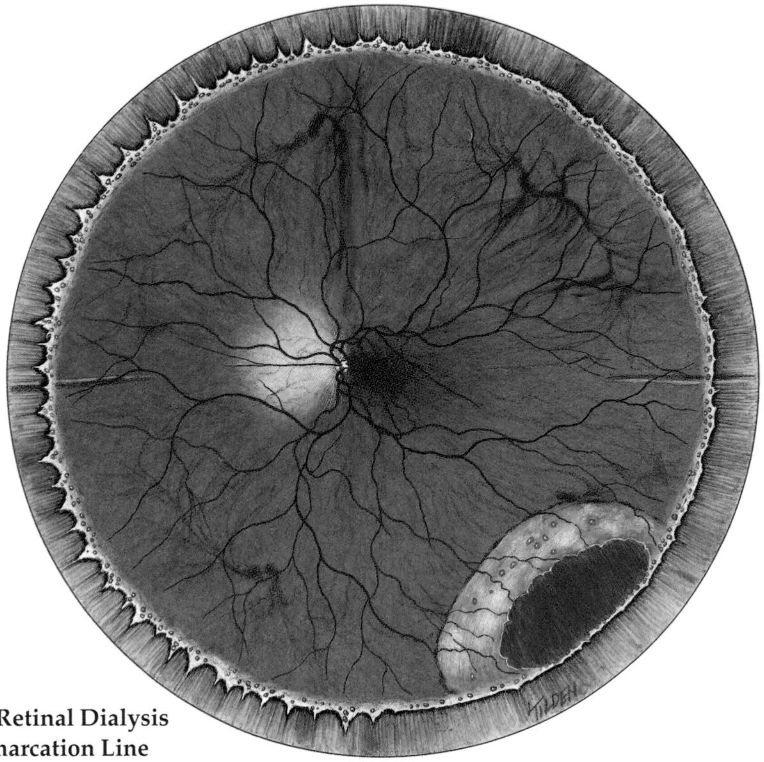

**Juvenile Retinal Dialysis
with Demarcation Line**

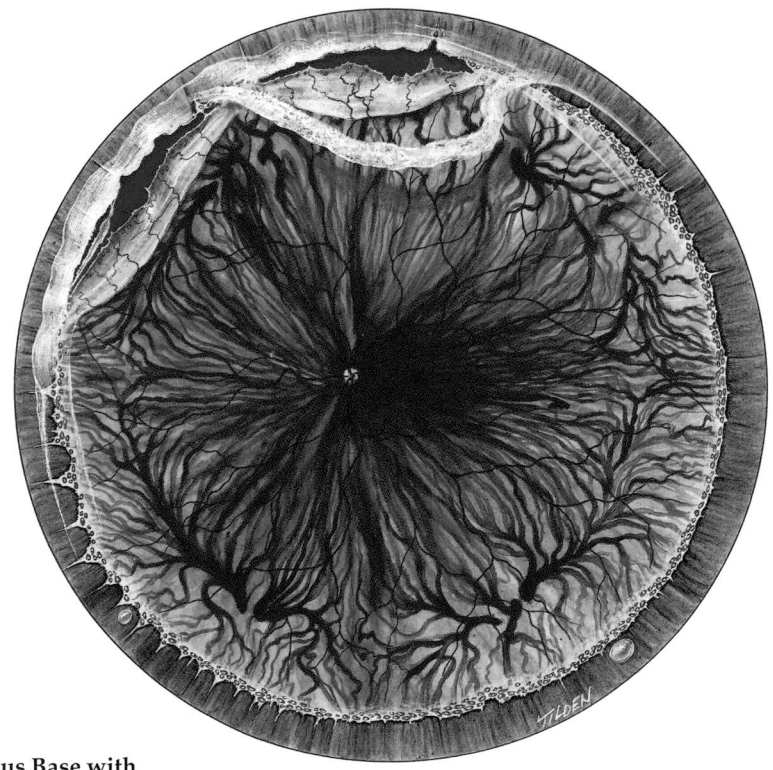

**Avulsion of Vitreous Base with
Retinal Dialysis and Early Retinal Detachment**

Giant Retinal Tears

Giant retinal tears are tears greater than 90° in circumferential length and may be spontaneous or due to trauma (20%). Thirty percent of cases occur in aphakic eyes. High myopes with lattice degeneration are especially at risk. Spontaneous cases, usually in males, occur without any warning. Twenty percent of cases have a familial history of retinal detachment. On occasion, giant retinal tears have been seen with colobomas of the lens-zonule system.

Giant retinal tears occur near the ora serrata, and usually there is a thin zone of elevated retina remaining attached at the ora serrata. There is a tendency for the giant tear flap to roll posteriorly and scroll up, in contrast to a retinal dialysis flap, which does not tend to fold posteriorly. The surgical and visual prognosis is extremely poor in giant retinal tears, whereas it is quite good in retinal dialyses. There is a high percentage of bilaterality in giant retinal tears.

Intrabasal Full-Thickness Retinal Tears

Intrabasal full-thickness retinal tears are located within the vitreous base and usually result from either a subtotal or complete avulsion of a preexisting retinal zonular traction tuft. There is no relationship of these tears to tractional forces acting along the posterior border of the vitreous base or to those forces created by a posterior cortical vitreous detachment. In addition, these tears do not appear to be related to advancing age, lattice degeneration, or trauma. Intrabasal full-thickness tears are rare and infrequently lead to retinal detachment.

Juxtabasal Full-Thickness Retinal Tears

Juxtabasal full-thickness retinal tears are invariably due to asymmetric tractional forces distributed along the posterior border of the vitreous base during an active posterior cortical vitreous detachment. These tears are almost always associated with a retinal flap and are the most common of the full-thickness retinal tears and carry the highest risk of developing a retinal detachment. Developmental variations and lattice retinal degeneration lesions create irregularities at the posterior border of the vitreous base and are therefore predisposing lesions for the development of juxtabasal full-thickness tears during a posterior cortical vitreous detachment. These lesions allow unequal distribution of tractional forces during the vitreous detachment process.

Extrabasal Full-Thickness Retinal Tears

Avulsions of cystic retinal tufts are often associated with a free vitreous operculum and represent the classic *extrabasal full-thickness retinal tear* which usually occurs in association with a posterior cortical vitreous detachment. These tears are not as common as the juxtabasal full-thickness retinal tears. On occasion, equatorial lattice retinal degeneration lesions may, in the presence of a posterior vitreous detachment, lead to the formation of an extrabasal full-thickness retinal tear. Pure extrabasal full-thickness operculated retinal tears do not, as a rule, produce total retinal detachments, but can lead to a localized retinal detachment usually one to two disc diameters in size.

Full-Thickness Peripheral Retinal Tears   **Plate 23**

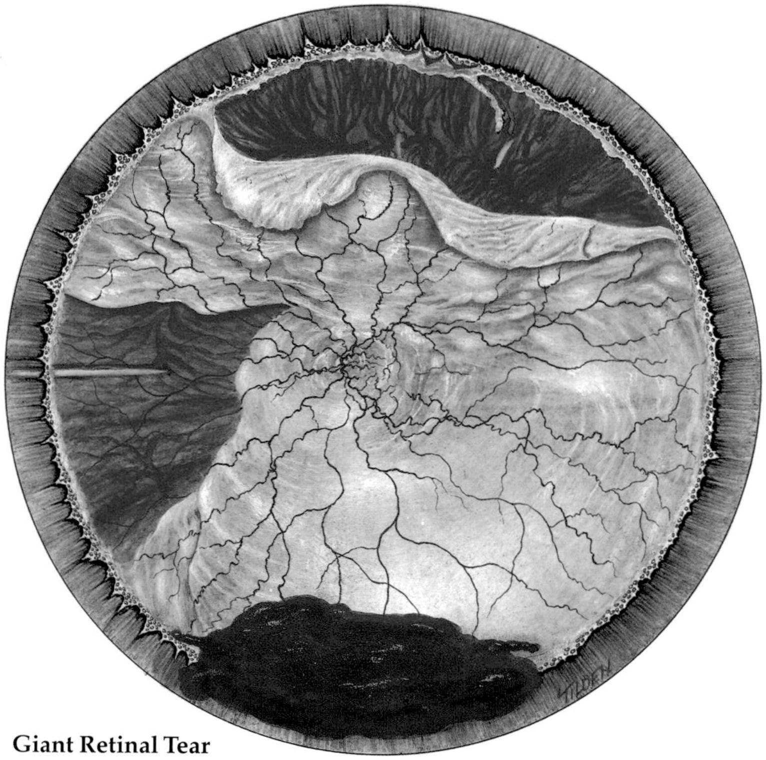

Giant Retinal Tear

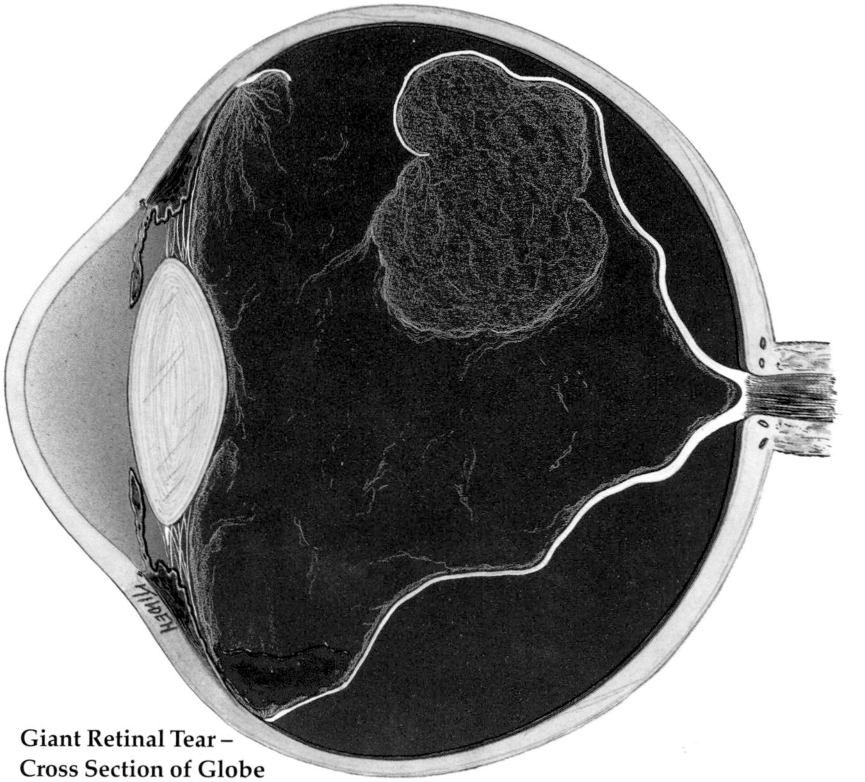

**Giant Retinal Tear –
Cross Section of Globe**

Full Thickness Retinal Tears

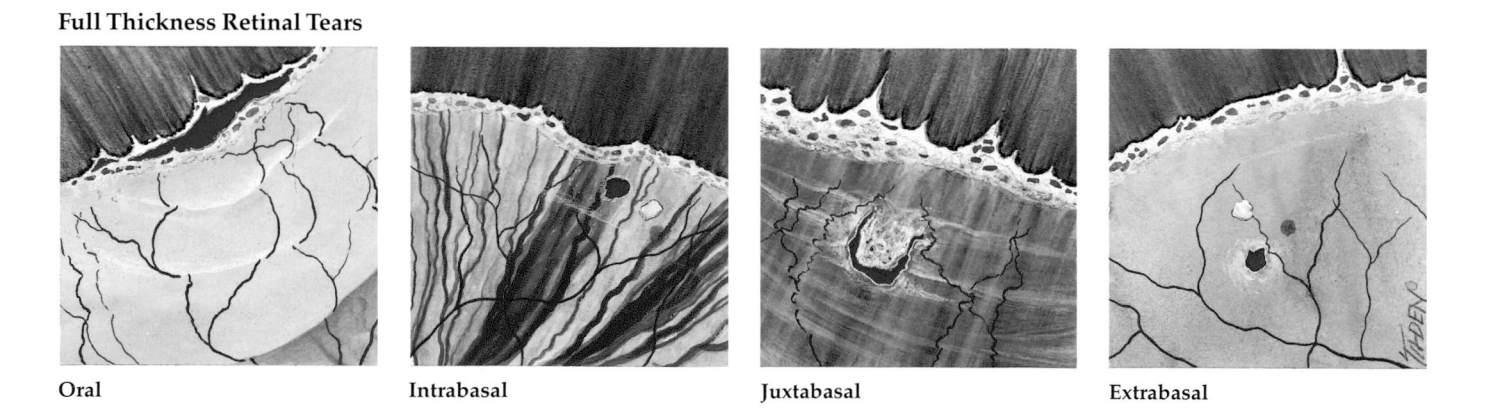

Oral   Intrabasal   Juxtabasal   Extrabasal

Trophic and Tractional Retinal Degenerations

6

The disorders in this section have trophic (nutritional and/or vascular) and tractional components that play a major role in their pathogenesis (see Table 6.1).

Table 6.1.
Trophic and Tractional Retinal Degenerations
White-without-pressure
White-with-pressure
Snail-track degeneration
Lattice retinal degeneration

Hereditary vitreoretinal degenerations
  Wagner's hereditary vitreoretinal degeneration
  Stickler's syndrome
  Congenital hereditary retinoschisis (juvenile)
  Goldmann-Favre disease
  Familial exudative vitreoretinopathy
  Snowflake degeneration

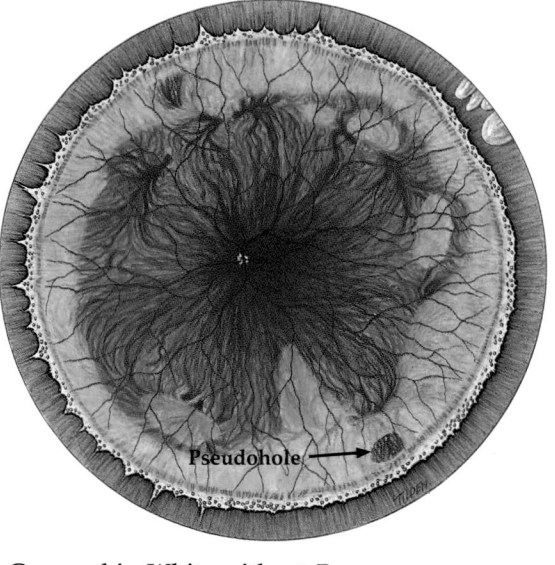

Geographic, White-without-Pressure

White-with- or -without-Pressure

White-without-Pressure

Normally the peripheral fundus is transparent when viewed with an indirect ophthalmoscope. When scleral depression is applied, there is no change in the transparency of the retina in the region of the scleral depression. However, in some individuals the retina appears translucent as a result of the scleral depression, and this has been termed white-with-pressure.

White-without-pressure refers to areas of peripheral retina that have a whitish translucent watered-silk appearance without scleral depression. The etiology of this condition remains obscure but may be related to vitreous traction. White-without-pressure is found more frequently in myopes and in dark-skinned people, for example, Negroes and people from the Mediterranean region. Often there are sharply demarcated edges to these geographic-shaped lesions. The lesions are usually located between the ora serrata and the equator. Often white-without-pressure lesions can be found posterior to the equator.

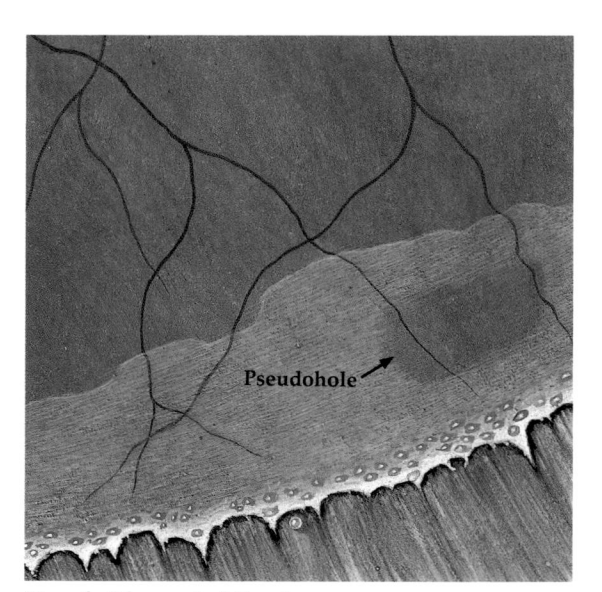

**Deeply Pigmented Fundus,
White-without-Pressure, Pseudohole**

Histopathology findings in regions of white-without-pressure include localized vitreoretinal adhesions, retinal atrophy of nuclear layers, cystoid degeneration, hyalinization of retinal arterioles, vitreous syneresis cavities, and posterior vitreous detachments. There does not appear to be any association of white-without-pressure lesions with retinal holes, tears, or retinal detachments.

White-with-Pressure

White-with-pressure is a whitish translucent bandlike lesion of the peripheral retinal usually located between the ora serrata and the equator. When the scleral depressor is applied to the outer surface of the globe, there is an indentation of the wall of the eye, and the retina goes from a transparent state to an opalescent state with some obscuration of the subjacent retinal pigment epithelium and choroidal vasculature. The borders of white-with-pressure have complex contours (geographic) and on occasion may even partially or completely surround a small region of normal retina which may be mistaken for a retinal hole, but it is really a pseudoretinal hole.

White-with-pressure should be differentiated from a flat

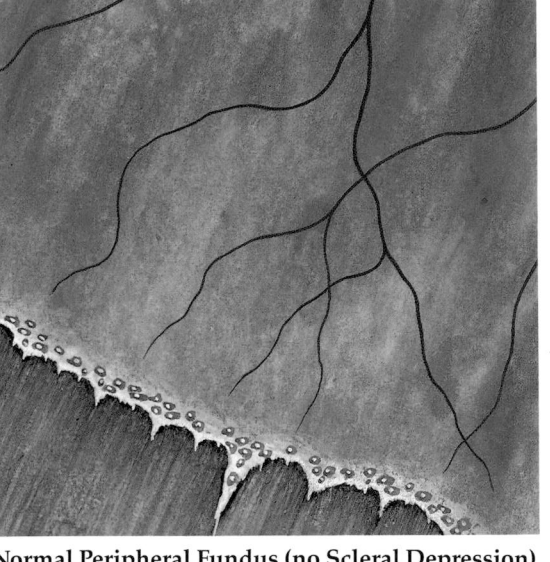
Normal Peripheral Fundus (no Scleral Depression)

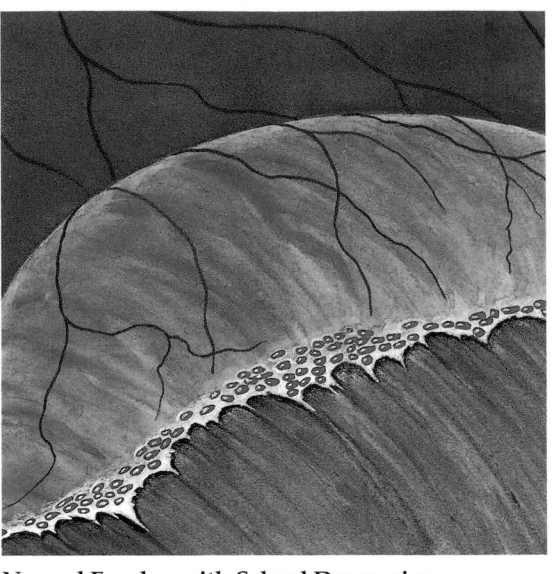
Normal Fundus with Scleral Depression

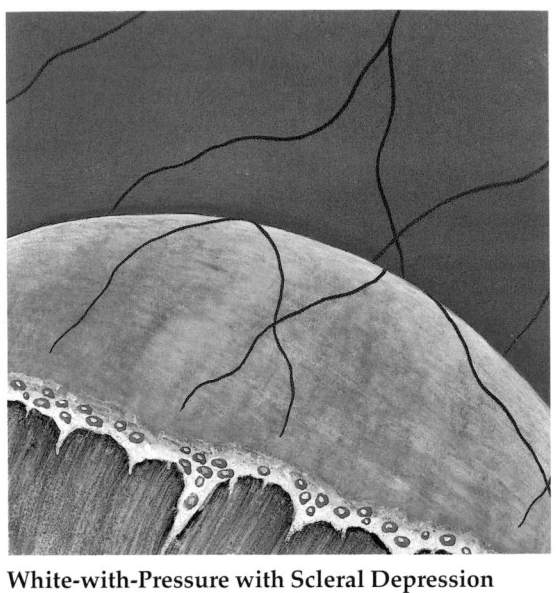
White-with-Pressure with Scleral Depression

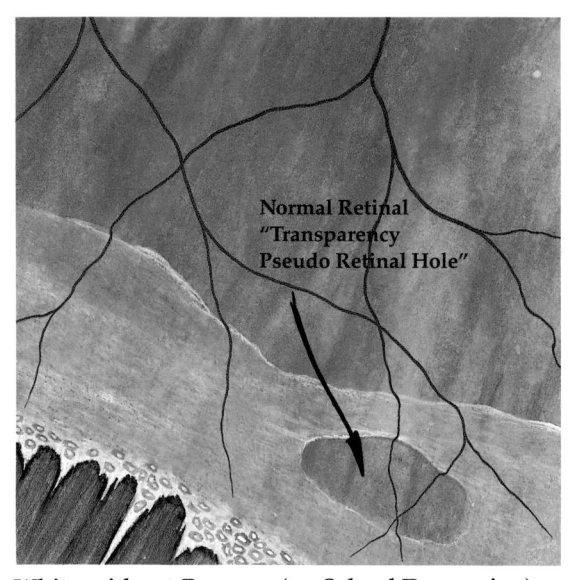
White-without-Pressure (no Scleral Depression)

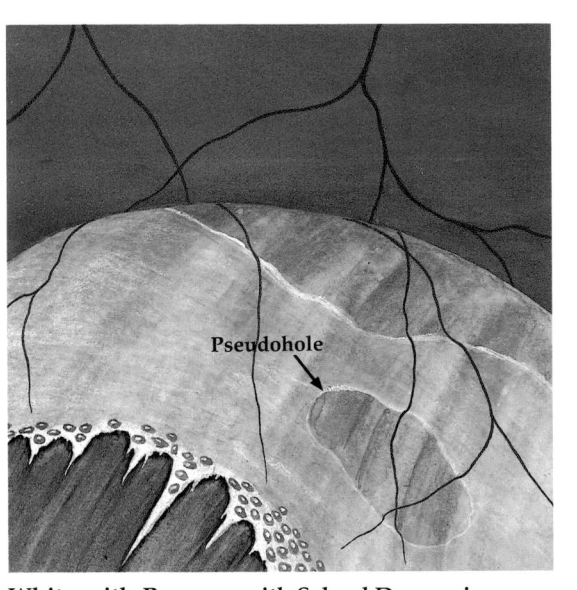
White-with-Pressure with Scleral Depression

or shallow retinal detachment, extensive cystoid degeneration, and flat degenerative retinoschisis lesions. White-with-pressure is also often seen at the edges of lattice retinal degeneration and cystoid degeneration.

The origin of white-with-pressure is still not well established, but may represent a weakness in the extracellular substance located in the subretinal space between the retinal pigment epithelium and the outer segments of the photoreceptor cells.

The incidence of white-with-pressure is over 30% of adult eyes and most cases are bilateral. Only 5% of people under 20 years of age have white-with-pressure, whereas 66% of those over 70 years of age have white-with-pressure. There is increased incidence of white-with-pressure with increased myopia, and the incidence approaches 100% in eyes with an anteroposterior or axial length of 33 mm or greater. It is more common in darkly pigmented fundi. Males are equally affected with this condition as are females. There is a predilection for the peripheral retina in the temporal quadrants and white-with-pressure lesions do not appear to be associated with retinal breaks.

Snail-Track Retinal Degeneration

Snail-track degeneration has been described as a variation or early stage of lattice retinal degeneration by some authors, while others have felt that it is a closely related, yet separate entity. Snail-track degeneration, or *"Schneckenspuren"* as Gonin termed it, consists of sharply demarcated bands of thin neurosensory retinal tissue, which have a crinkled or frosted appearance on their inner surface.

Characteristically, white vessel or lattice changes as well as retinal pigment abnormalities (deposits) are absent in snail-track degeneration, in contrast to lattice retinal degeneration. Retinal holes without opercula are found in snail-track degeneration in the following quadrantic distribution: inferotemporal quadrant 54%, superotemporal quadrant 18%, superonasal quadrant 16% and the inferonasal quadrant 12%. There is syneresis of the vitreous gel in affected eyes in 100% of cases and the incidence of retinal detachments in these eyes has been reported as high as 48%.

In these cases, 80% of the snail-track lesions are located within the anterior half of the peripheral retina; 90% are in myopic eyes, with 33% in highly myopic eyes. Snail-track degeneration lesions have a predilection for the superonasal and superotemporal quadrants. There is an autosomal recessive transmission tendency, and males and females are equally affected.

Snail-Track Retinal Degeneration   **Plate 25**

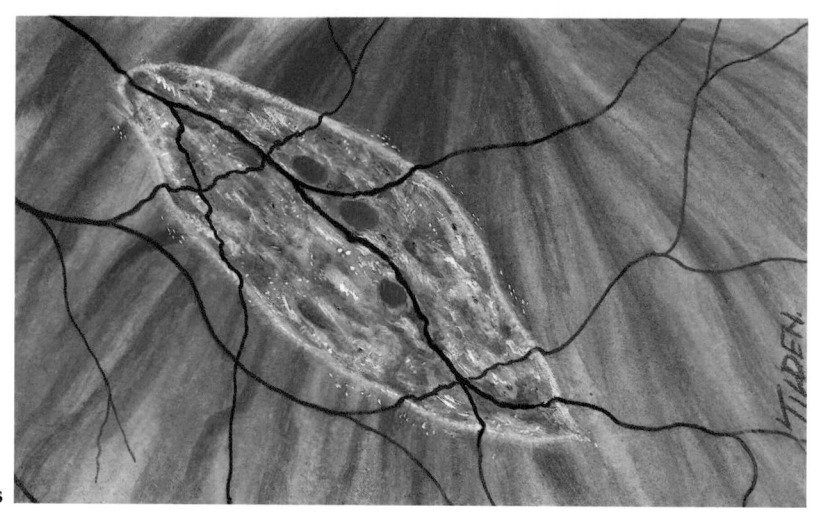

Snail-Track Degeneration – Fundus

Snail-Track Degeneration – Cross Section:
Liquefaction of Vitreous over Snail-Track
Lesion

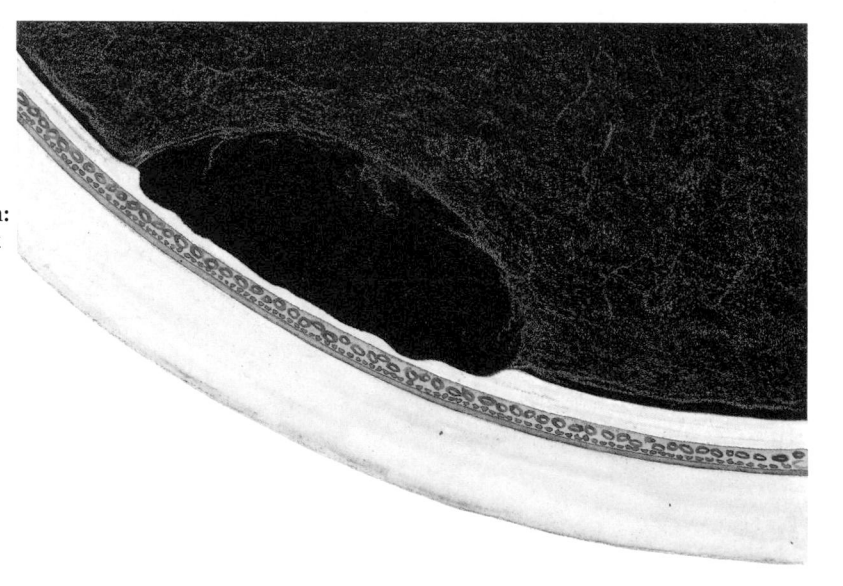

Lattice Retinal Degeneration

Gonin was the first to describe *Schneckenspuren* in 1904, which was later renamed lattice retinal degeneration in the 1950s. *Lattice retinal degeneration* consists of a sharply demarcated circumferentially oriented lesion characterized by thinning of the inner portion (vitreal) of the neurosensory retina, white lines, and a pigmentary disturbance. There is an arborizing network of "sheathed" retinal vessels due to an obliterative fibrosis reaction, which is seen ophthalmoscopically as a series of white lines crisscrossing one another. Schepens coined the term "lattice" to describe this network of white blood vessels within the lesion site. Lattice retinal vessels are present in about 46% of cases. In 92% of the cases a pigmentary disturbance is found in the subjacent retinal pigment epithelium, consisting of depigmentation zones and clumps of hyperpigmentation as well as perivascular pigmentation of neurosensory retina within the lattice degeneration lesion.

There is a focal thinning of the inner portion of the retina with loss of retinal neurons and thinning of the internal limiting membrane. Sometimes there are areas where the internal limiting membrane is absent, and glial cells manufacture additional internal limiting (basement) membrane, which is seen ophthalmoscopically as greyish-white particles on the inner surface of the lattice lesions. Invariably, there is liquefaction of the vitreous over the lattice lesions with abnormal vitreoretinal attachments at the margins of the lattice lesions. Retinal tear sites, when they develop, tend to do so along the margins of the lattice degeneration lesion.

Most lattice lesions are found anterior to the equator and two thirds of them are in the vertical meridians between the 11 o'clock and 1 o'clock meridians superiorly and between the 5 o'clock and 7 o'clock meridians inferiorly. The major axis of the lattice lesion is oriented parallel to the equator and is termed *equatorial lattice degeneration* (68%). Radial (7%) or paravascular lattice degeneration (parallels retinal vessels) is less common than the equatorial type and is located more posteriorly. There is focal thinning (19.2%) of the inner portion of the neurosensory retina and round or oval retinal holes are noted in 18.2 to 31.0% of cases. Retinal tears are found in 1.4% of eyes with lattice degeneration, and for the most part these are situated at the lateral or posterior edges of the lattice lesion.

Of all retinal detachments, lattice degeneration lesions are present in 41% of cases, and it is thought that lattice degeneration is the major cause of the detachment process in 21% of cases. In 55 to 70% of these cases, a tear developing at the posterior or lateral border of the lattice lesion is responsible for the detachment, whereas in 30 to 45% of cases atrophic holes within the lattice lesion are responsible for the development of the retinal detachment. Most of the patients who develop retinal detachments due to lattice degeneration are over 50 years of age, and 43% of these eyes are myopic.

The overall incidence of lattice degeneration is from 6 to 7.9% of the adult population, with males and females equally affected. The onset is usually in the second decade of life and tends to be bilateral in 33 to 50% of cases. Lattice degeneration is more common in myopic eyes than in hyperopic eyes. The incidence of lattice retinal degeneration increases with increasing axial length of the globe. There is usually no hereditary pattern in lattice retinal degeneration; however, in some families an autosomal dominant transmission has been mapped out.

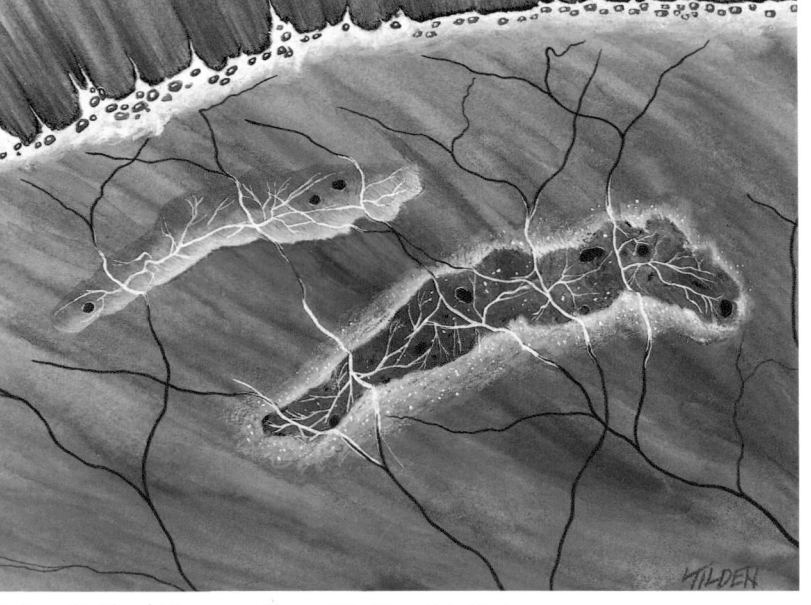

Lattice Retinal Degeneration with Atrophic Holes

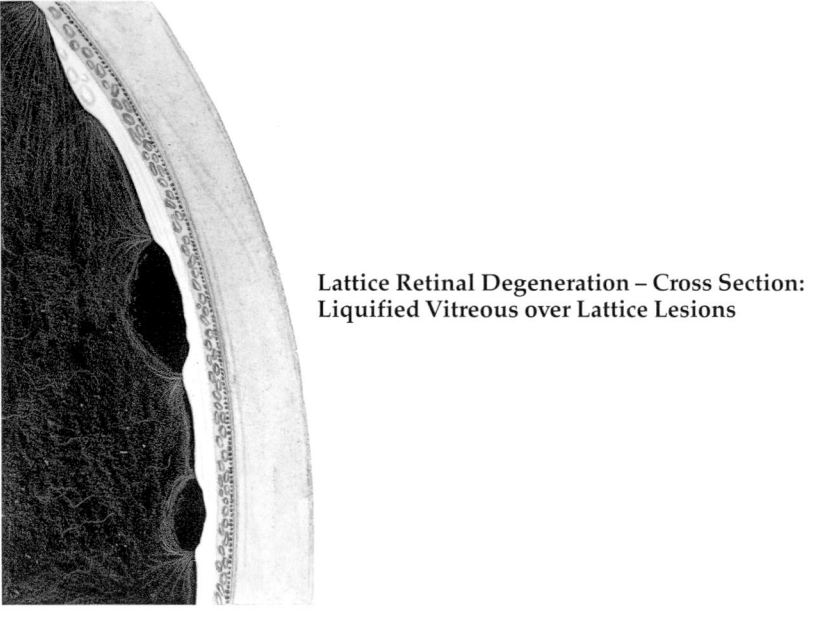

**Lattice Retinal Degeneration – Cross Section:
Liquified Vitreous over Lattice Lesions**

**Lattice Degeneration with Horseshoe Tears
and Localized Retinal Detachment**

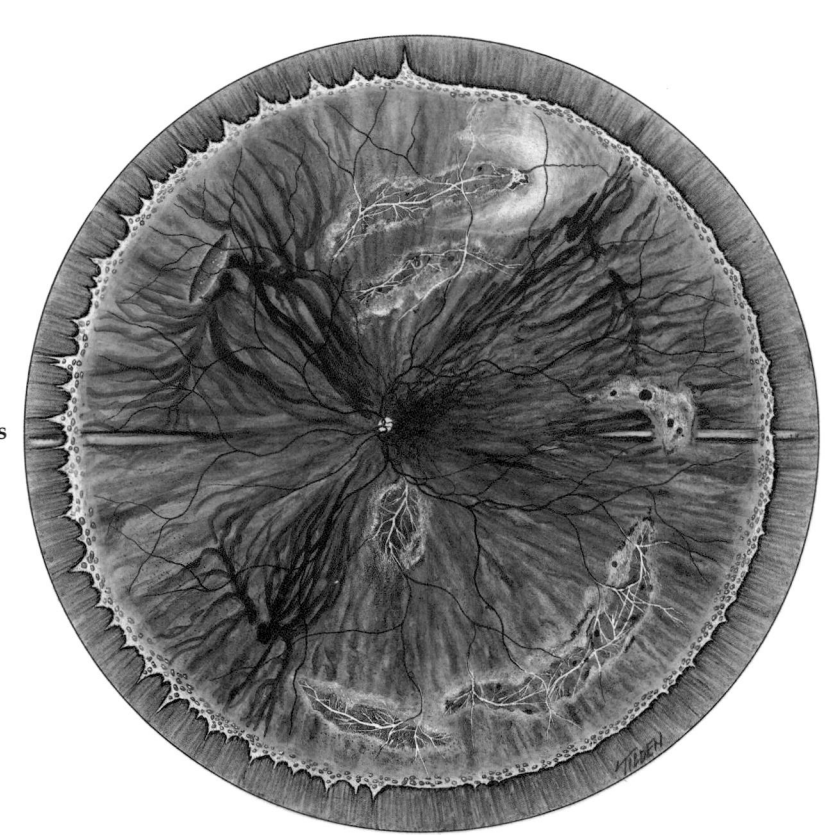

Plate 27   **Wagner's Hereditary Vitreoretinal Degeneration**

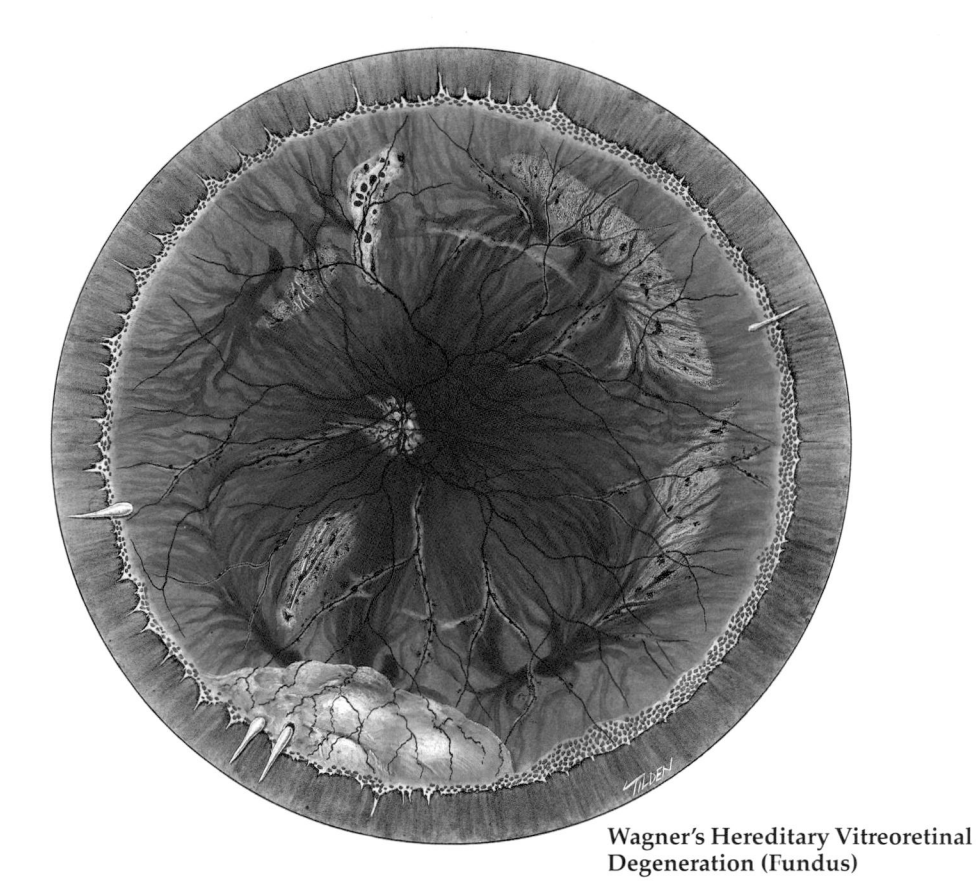

Wagner's Hereditary Vitreoretinal
Degeneration (Fundus)

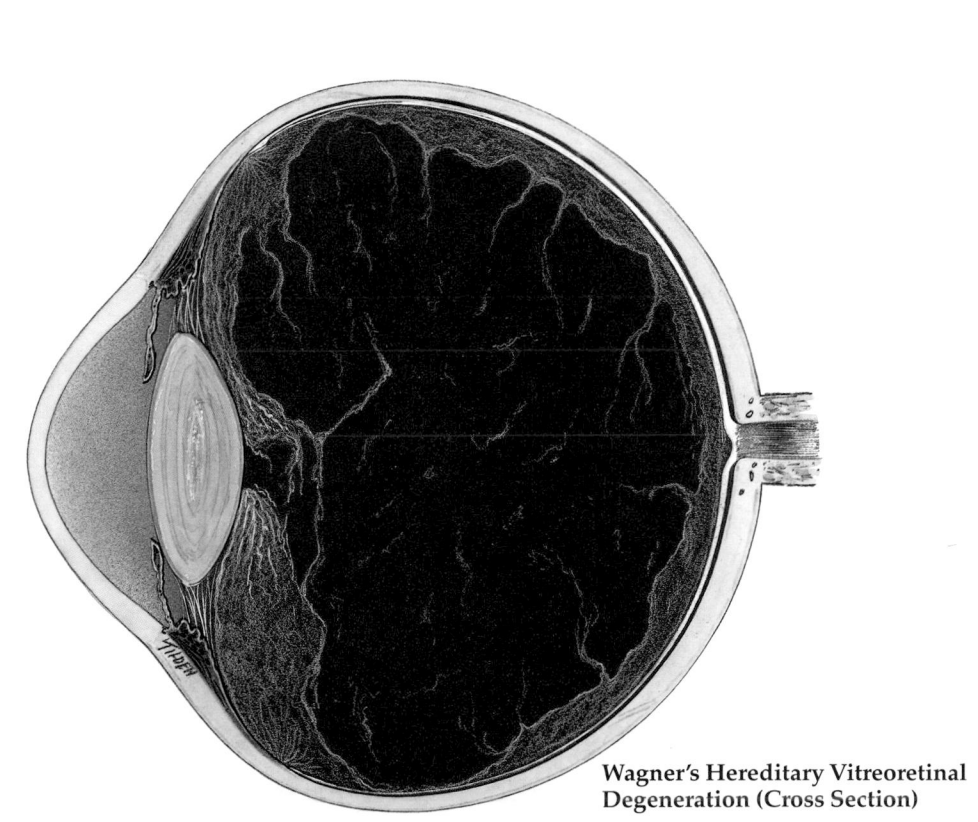

Wagner's Hereditary Vitreoretinal
Degeneration (Cross Section)

Hereditary Vitreoretinal Degenerations

Hereditary vitreoretinal degenerations consist of a group of disorders primarily affecting the vitreous and retina with a distinct hereditary pattern and are listed in Table 6.1. Systemic disorders associated with some of the vitreoretinal degenerations are enumerated in Table 6.2.

Table 6.1. Hereditary Vitreoretinal Degenerations
Wagner's hereditary vitreoretinal degeneration
Stickler's syndrome
Congenital hereditary retinoschisis (juvenile)
Goldmann-Favre's disease
Familial exudative vitreoretinopathy
Snowflake degeneration

Table 6.2. Systemic Conditions Associated with Vitreoretinal Degenerations
Marfan's syndrome
Homocystinuria
Ehlers-Danlos syndrome
Pseudoxanthoma elasticum

Wagner's Hereditary Vitreoretinal Degeneration

Wagner first described this hereditary vitreoretinal degeneration in 1938. Characteristically, there is a large syneresis cavity behind the lens with membranous condensations of the vitreous body (bands and veils). There is a high incidence of cataracts and retinal detachment in this autosomal dominant disease, which is usually bilateral. Retinal vessels are narrowed and sheathed with paravascular pigmentation, and there is retinal pigment epithelium atrophy, choroidal atrophy, and, in some cases, optic atrophy. The electroretinogram is understandably subnormal. There is often radial and equatorial lattice degeneration, peripheral degenerative retinoschisis, myopia, and glaucoma found in the eyes of patients with Wagner's hereditary vitreoretinal degeneration (see Table 6.3).

Stickler's Syndrome

In 1965, Stickler described a hereditary progressive arthroophthalmopathy, with associated cleft palate, high myopia (−16 diopters), an optically empty vitreous cavity with fundus pigmentary abnormalities, preretinal membranes, cataracts, and a malignant form of retinal detachment that had an autosomal dominant inheritance pattern. Other systemic findings that have been attributed to Stickler's syndrome include flattened facies, skeletal dysplasia, and, on rare occasions, mental retardation.

The major ophthalmic and systemic abnormalities of Wagner's hereditary vitreoretinal degeneration and Stickler's syndrome are outlined in Table 6.3.

There is a high incidence of retinal detachments in patients with Wagner's disease and/or Stickler's syndrome, and they are difficult to repair because of the vitreoretinal membranes, cataracts, large (5% have giant retinal tears) and multiple retinal tears, and an increased tendency to go on to massive periretinal proliferation. Many cases need vitrectomy in addition to scleral buckling surgery to repair the retinal detachment. The surgical success rate in these cases has been reported to be 68%.

Table 6.3.

Wagner's Hereditary Vitreoretinal Degeneration

Ophthalmic findings
  Large syneresis cavities
  Large lacunae (central and posterior vitreous)
  Vitreous veils (membranous condensations)
  Retinal vessels narrowed
  Retinal vessels sheathed
  Paravascular retinal pigmentation (periphery) (61%)
  Choroidal vessel atrophy (40%)
    Hyperpigmentation
    Hypopigmentation
  Tessellated fundus
  Retinal detachment (50%)
  Atypical posterior vitreous detachments
  Retinal breaks (75%)
  Lattice retinal degeneration (26%)
  Retinoschisis
  Cataracts (after adolescence, 60% incidence)
    Posterior capsular (41%)
    Posterior subcapsular (31%)
    Nuclear sclerosis (28%)
    Mature cataract (28%)
  Optic atrophy (4%)
  Contracted visual fields (ring scotoma)
  Subnormal electroretinogram (ERG)
  Night blindness
  Color vision – normal
  Dark adaptation – decreased
  Glaucoma
  Myopia
  Epicanthus
  Extensive white-with-pressure (35%)
  Meridional folds (17%)

Systemic manifestations (Stickler's syndrome)
  Arthropathy
  Cleft palate
  Flat nose
  Genu valgum
  Micrognathia
  Glossoptosis
  Chondrodysplasia

Congenital Hereditary Retinoschisis (Juvenile Retinoschisis)

Congenital hereditary retinoschisis involves a splitting of the retina at the nerve fiber layer into an inner and outer layer of retina, which results in absolute scotomas in the visual field corresponding to the zones of schisis. Congenital retinoschisis is most frequently observed in the inferotemporal quadrant and can extend to the posterior pole, but does not, as a rule, extend to the ora serrata region.

Vitreous findings in congenital retinoschisis include a larger than usual Cloquet's canal (early cases with infantile canal proportions) and a prominent fibrous condensation of the cortex. In advanced cases, vitreous bands are found crisscrossing the vitreous gel, which shows widespread nonconfluent liquefaction cavities. The vitreous cortex is usually attached to the inner surface of the retinoschisis cavity and is liquefied over the region of a retinal break in the inner layer. Incomplete posterior vitreous detachment with a collapse of the cortex is frequently observed in cases of retinoschisis, showing giant inner layer holes with a history of recurrent vitreous hemorrhage. Vitreous traction on the retinal vessels may lead to a massive vitreous hemorrhage.

Congenital retinoschisis is usually discovered in children and young adults, but has been detected at birth. Most of the patients see floaters and have poor vision with strabismus or nystagmus. Congenital retinoschisis is invariably bilateral and is transmitted as a sex-linked recessive mode of inheritance. In rare cases, it has been found in females as an autosomal recessive disease.

During the first five years of life, there is usually progression (increased volume of retinoschisis, increased numbers of inner and/or outer layer breaks) and then it levels off and is fairly stable by the age of 20. There are periods of regression usually associated with release of vitreous cortical traction on the inner surface of the retina. The ophthalmoscopic features of congenital retinoschisis are outlined as follows:*

> *Inner layer* is extremely thin, elevated with a smooth dome or balloon shape and is immobile. Retinal vessels are often sheathed and are seen on its inner surface. Inner

* Modified from Tolentino FI, Schepens CL, Freeman HM: Vitreoretinal Disorders/Diagnosis and Management. Philadelphia, W.B. Saunders Company, 1976, pp 251, 254.

layer breaks are often multiple, round or oval, and quite variable in size. In some cases the holes are so large that only the vessels and minimal amounts of atrophic retina are left behind. Gliosis and neovascularization of the inner layer have been observed.

> *Outer layer* is often invisible when it is attached and becomes visible with detachment. The outer layer contains strands of Müller's cells and is avascular. Outer layer breaks are oval and have rolled edges.

> *Optic disc:* pseudopapillitis, pseudopapilledema, "dragging of the disc" and optic-disc pallor (atrophy) have been noted in congenital retinoschisis.

> *Macula* shows cystic retinal changes, giving the appearance of a depigmented star on a background of mottled pigment (beaten copper). This may represent an incomplete form of retinoschisis within the macula that results from a peripheral schisis extension into the macula. Less often, there is independent schisis developing in the macula.

Histopathologic analysis reveals that the splitting takes place at the nerve fiber layer of the retina in congenital retinoschisis, as compared to acquired typical degenerative retinoschisis where the split takes place in the outer plexiform layer. The vitreous cortex is adherent to the inner retinal layer of congenital retinoschisis, and the retinoschisis cavity contains an amorphous proteinaceous material. The vitreous cavity is smaller than normal, and the vitreous gel is located anterior to the inner layer of retinoschisis. Fibrous metaplasia of the macular retinal pigment epithelium is often present.

There is no satisfactory form of treatment for congenital retinoschisis that will restore vision lost from the damaged neurosensory retina at the schisis lesion sites. However, if outer layer breaks are present, photocoagulation or cryosurgery may be of some value. If a retinal detachment develops, then scleral buckling surgery and an encircling band are appropriate. The goal of such surgery would be to close all the outer layer breaks.

The differential diagnosis of congenital retinoschisis includes retinal detachment, acquired typical and reticular degenerative retinoschisis, Eales' disease, retinitis pigmentosa, sickle cell retinopathy, retrolental fibroplasia (cicatricial stage), and persistent hyperplastic primary vitreous.

Congenital Hereditary Retinoschisis   **Plate 28**
(Juvenile Retinoschisis)

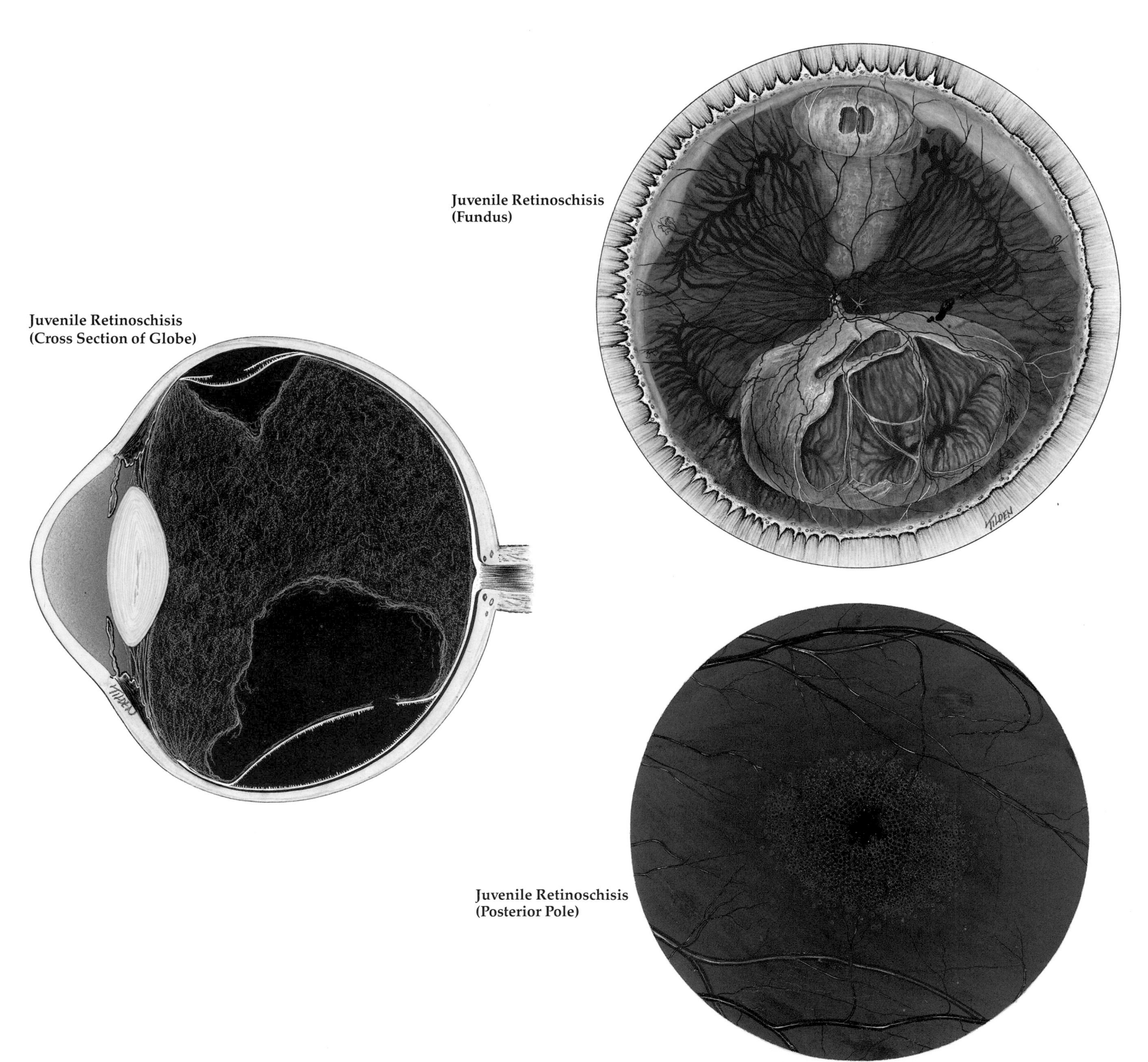

Juvenile Retinoschisis
(Fundus)

Juvenile Retinoschisis
(Cross Section of Globe)

Juvenile Retinoschisis
(Posterior Pole)

Goldmann-Favre Disease

Goldmann-Favre disease is characterized by peripheral and macular retinoschisis, retinitis pigmentosa-like retinal changes, an optically empty vitreous cavity with vitreous veils, radial lattice degeneration, night blindness, and cataracts (see Table 6.4). Goldmann-Favre's disease is inherited as an autosomal recessive trait and therefore affects males and females equally. The disease tends to be bilateral.

The peripheral (outer and inner layer holes) and macular retinoschisis as well as the pigmentary macular (beaten metal appearance) changes in Goldmann-Favre's disease closely resemble those described for congenital retinoschisis and are responsible for constricted visual fields and poor central vision (scotomas). The "bone-corpuscle" paravascular retinal pigmentation (equator and posterior pole regions) resemble the pigmentary findings in retinitis pigmentosa. A diminished or extinct electroretinogram is also present.

The vitreous shows considerable liquefaction with a large optically empty syneresis cavity similar to that found in Wagner's vitreoretinal degeneration. Pleated vitreal membranes and a thickened posterior cortical vitreous are present, resembling a preretinal membrane. The posterior cortex is usually adherent to the inner layer of retinoschisis and to the areas of chorioretinal pigmentary proliferation. Retinal detachments in Goldmann-Favre's disease have a poor prognosis, as noted in Wagner's degeneration and in Stickler's syndrome.

Table 6.4.

Goldmann-Favre Disease: Ophthalmic Findings

Optically empty vitreous

Absent posterior cortical vitreous detachment

Thickened posterior cortical vitreous

Congenital retinoschisis picture
  Inner layer retinal holes
  Outer layer retinal holes
  Retinal detachments

Retinitis pigmentosa picture
  Paravascular retinal pigmentation
  Diminished or extinquished ERG
  Chorioretinal atrophy

Complicated cataracts

Peripheral (congenital-type) retinoschisis

Macular retinoschisis
  Macular pigment changes (beaten metal)

Constricted visual fields

Central scotomas

Bilateral disease

Autosomal recessive (familial) transmission

Goldmann-Favre Disease   **Plate 29**

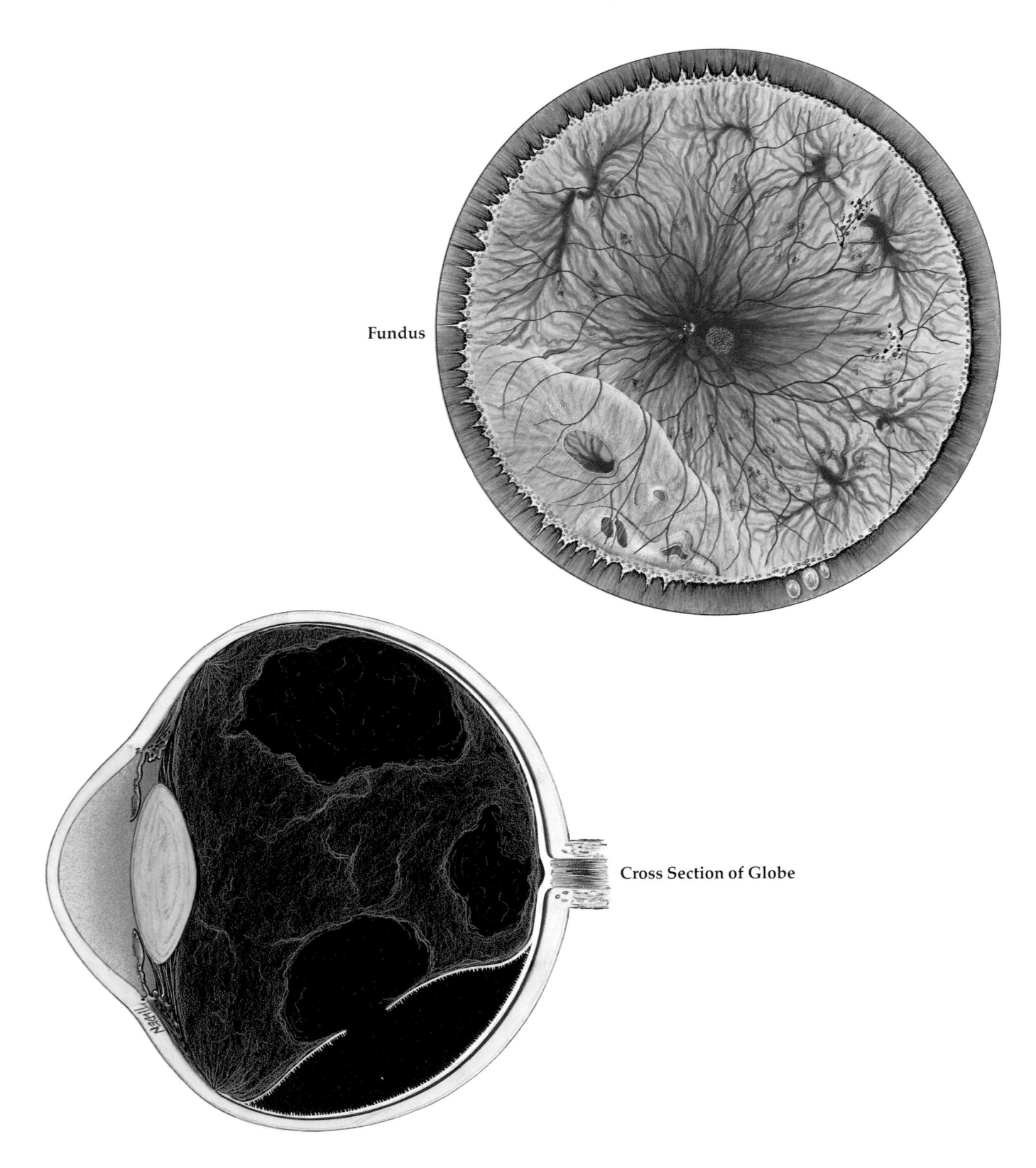

Fundus

Cross Section of Globe

Familial Exudative Vitreoretinopathy

Familial exudative vitreoretinopathy is an autosomal dominant disorder affecting young individuals who usually present with late signs, including cataract, strabismus, and nystagmus. Vitreous exudation is found throughout the vitreous gel. Vitreous contraction is the prominent feature of this
disorder and there is vitreous condensation in the vitreous
base and cortical regions. White-with-pressure and
peripheral cystoid degeneration are often present.

Liquefaction of the vitreous gel is an infrequent finding.
Posterior cortical vitreous detachments may be present, but
are not found in the optic nerve head and macular regions.
Contraction of the vitreous body is a constant finding. A
dragged disc may also be seen. The vitreous gel has a haze,
and sometimes it has a snowflake appearance. Often there
is a low-grade iridocyclitis with cells in the aqueous humor
and in the anterior vitreous, which are most likely due to vitreous traction on the ciliary body. Intravitreal bands can lead
to retinal tears with rolled edges.

In the advanced stages of this disease, tractional retinal
detachment, massive periretinal proliferation, and vitreous
hemorrhage are often seen. In addition, peripheral retinal
neovascularization may be responsible for recurrent vitreous hemorrhages. If a patient develops a rhegmatogenous
retinal detachment, scleral buckling surgery will be required. With a vitreous hemorrhage, a pars plana vitrectomy may also be indicated, but usually the surgical results
and visual prognosis in these patients are poor.

The differential diagnosis of familial exudative vitreoretinopathy includes retrolental fibroplasia, Coat's disease, Eales' disease, peripheral uveitis, angiomatosis re-
tinae, and posterior persistent hyperplastic primary vitreous.

Familial Exudative Vitreoretinopathy   **Plate 30**

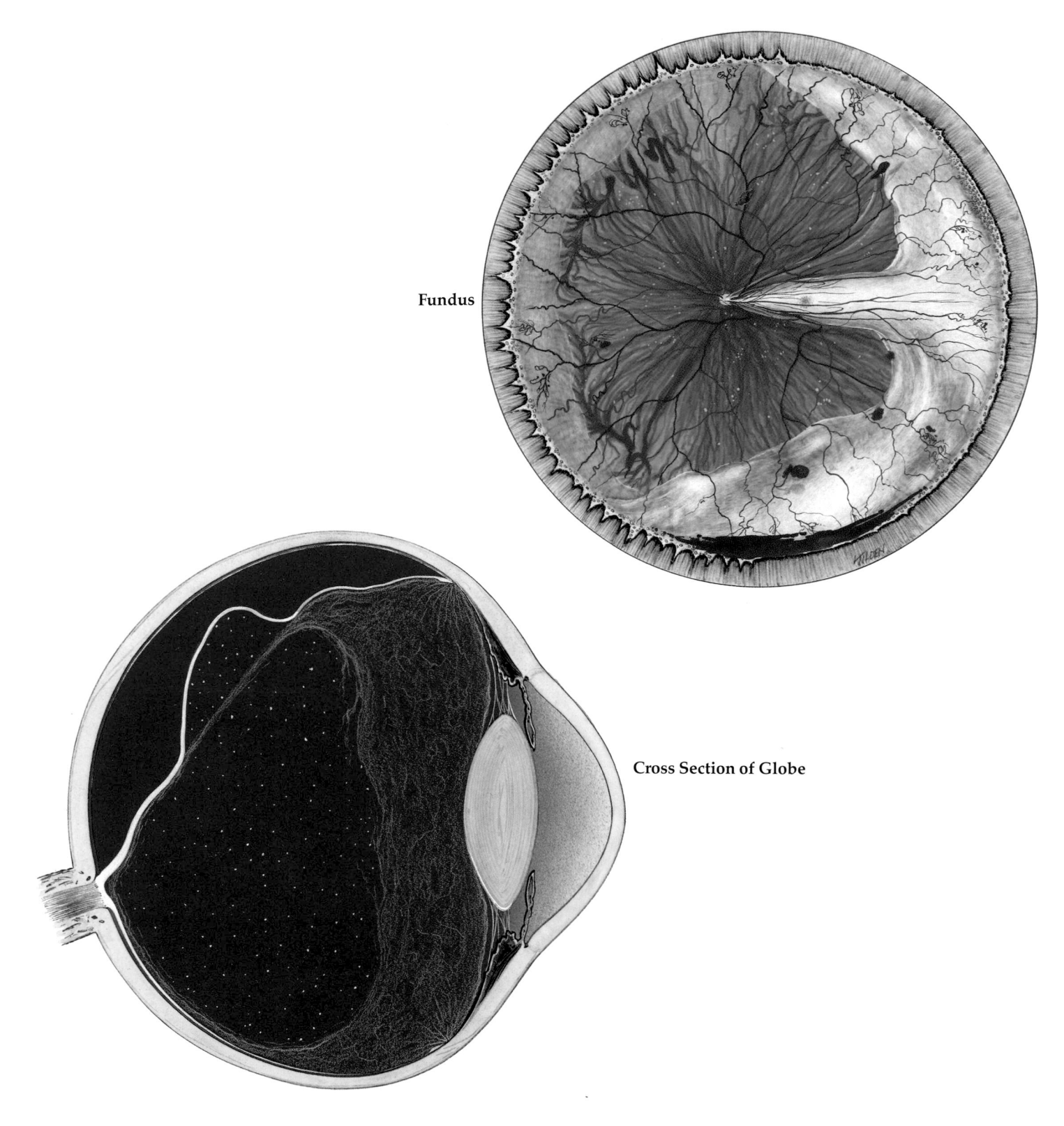

Fundus

Cross Section of Globe

Snowflake Vitreoretinal Degeneration

Snowflake hereditary vitreoretinal degeneration is a progressive disorder characterized by vitreous strands, syneresis of the vitreous, low-grade myopia, cataracts, and yellow retinal dots in areas of excessive white-with-pressure in the peripheral fundus. Retinal detachments in this disease are caused by multiple retinal breaks, usually at the equator in the temporal quadrants. The visual prognosis in these patients is often poor. Visual field depressions and reductions in the ERG scotopic b-wave amplitude as well as increased rod thresholds in dark-adaptation testing can be found in the later stages of snowflake vitreoretinal degeneration. The disease itself has been divided into the four stages listed in Table 6.5.

Table 6.5.
Snowflake Vitreoretinal Degeneration

Stage	Age (years)	Features
I	Under 15	Extensive white-with-pressure in fundus periphery
II	15–25	Minute snowflakes (yellowish dots) in areas of white-with-pressure; snowflakes are located on inner portion of neurosensory retina; decreased retinal transparency in region of snowflakes
		Snowflake distribution patterns: Anterior location — Snowflakes scattered around fundus periphery; Posterior location — Radial–paravascular; Equatorial–discrete areas parallel to the equator
		Snowflakes cratered with excavated centers (saucer-shaped) and thickened overlying vitreous
		↓ Dark adaptation (↑ rod threshold)
III	25–50	Retinal vessels are sheathed (white threads). There are pigment abnormalities (clumps of pigment) at posterior margins of snowflake craters
		Floating vitreous strands
		Cataracts
		ERG's (↓)
		Visual fields (↓)
IV	Over 60	Increased fundus pigmentation
		Retinal vessels may "disappear"
		Chorioretinal atrophy around previous pigment clumps
		Snowflakes less prominent
		Retina is atrophic; patients usually have surgical aphakia
		Night blindness

Abstracted with permission from Schepens CL: Retinal Detachment and Allied Diseases, Vol. 2, Philadelphia, W.B. Saunders Company, 1983, pp 614–615.

Snowflake Vitreoretinal Degeneration **Plate 31**

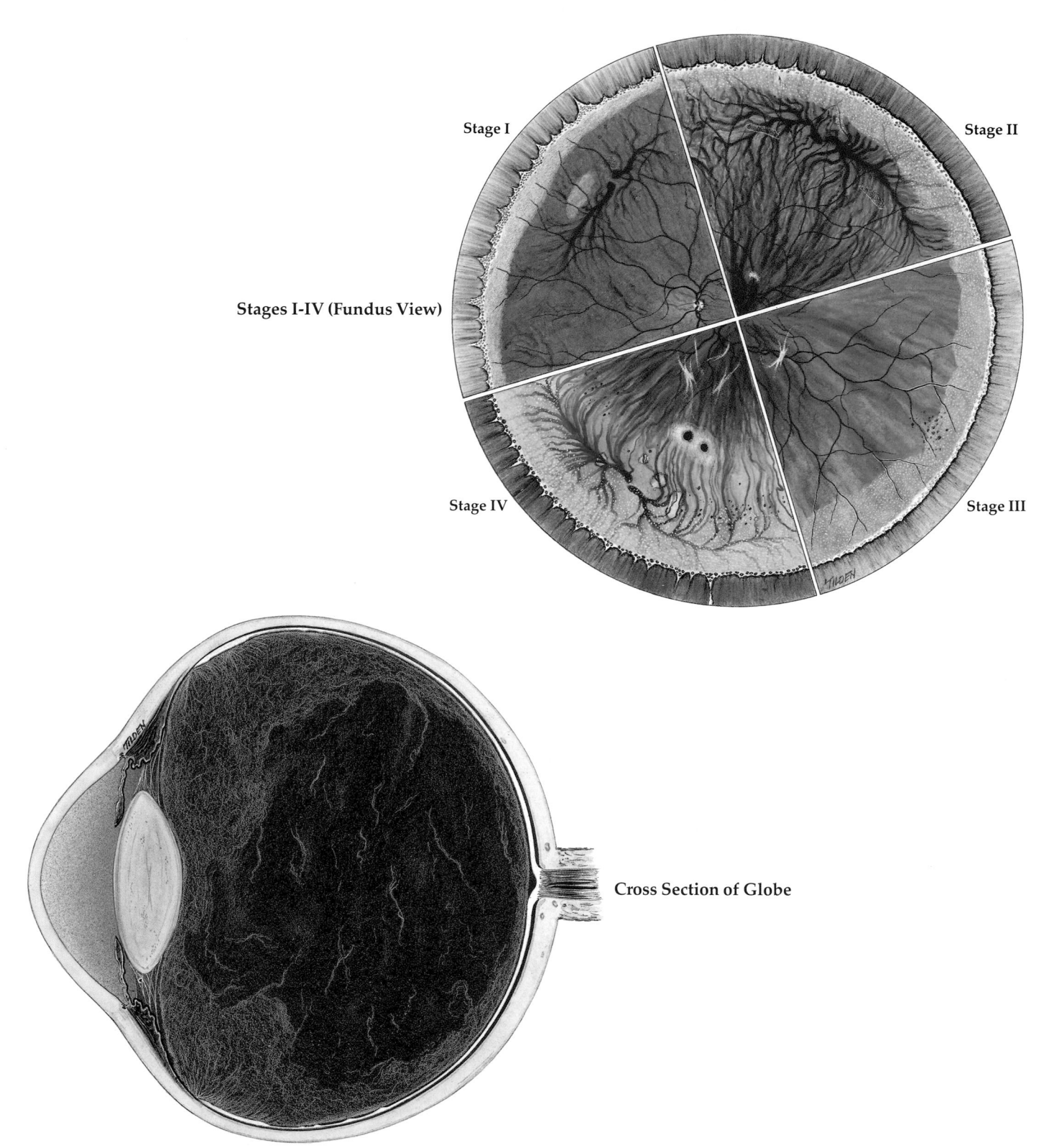

Stage I

Stage II

Stages I-IV (Fundus View)

Stage IV

Stage III

Cross Section of Globe

Systemic Conditions Associated With Vitreoretinal Degenerations

Marfan's Syndrome

Marfan's syndrome is characterized by arachnodactyly, connective tissue abnormalities such as aortic aneurysms, hypermobility of joints, and ectopia lentis. There is an autosomal dominant inheritance pattern, and males and females are affected equally. Most cases of Marfan's syndrome are caused by an inability of the tissues to incorporate hydroxyproline into specific proteins in a normal manner. In a small percentage (20%) of Marfan cases, the metabolic defect involves homocystine.

Patients with Marfan's syndrome often have high myopia and vitreous and lattice degeneration with associated retinal breaks commonly located in the equatorial region, which predispose the affected eyes to develop retinal detachments. Removal of subluxated or dislocated lenses in Marfan's patients is frequently accompanied by vitreous loss, which, in turn, further increases the chances of developing a retinal detachment. Frequently their pupils fail to dilate well, and, along with subluxation of their lenses, it is difficult to get a clear view of the retinal periphery using indirect ophthalmoscopy. Marfan's patients also have anterior chamber angle abnormalities and are predisposed to open-angle glaucoma.

Marfan's Syndrome   Plate 32

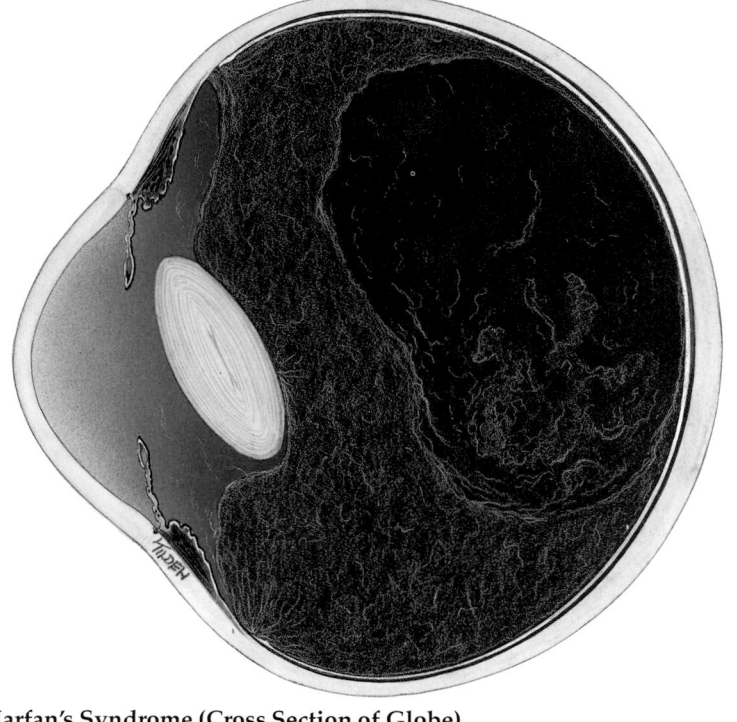

Marfan's Syndrome (Cross Section of Globe)
– Subluxated Lens

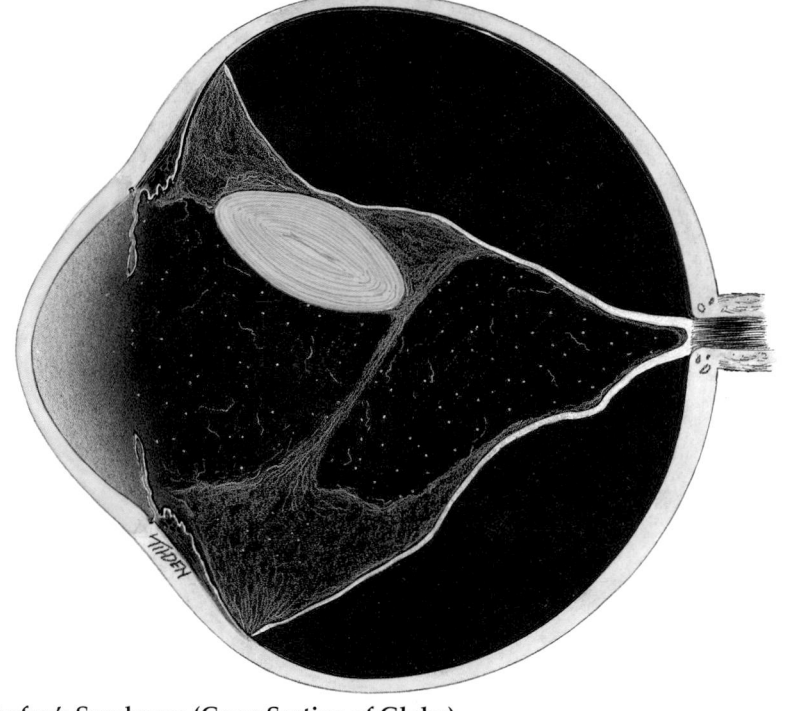

Marfan's Syndrome (Cross Section of Globe)
– Subluxated Lens with Retinal Detachment

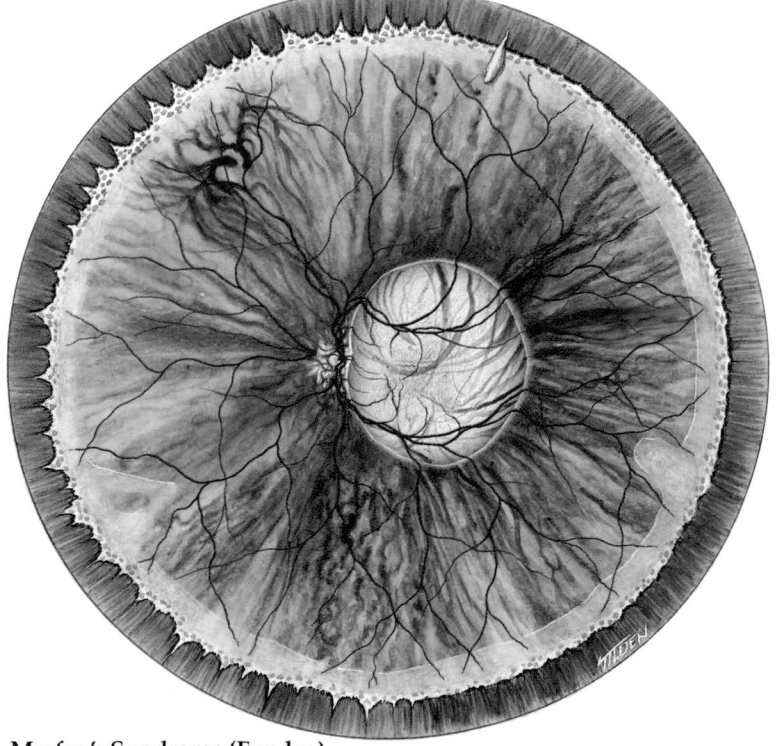

Marfan's Syndrome (Fundus)
– Myopia with Posterior Staphyloma

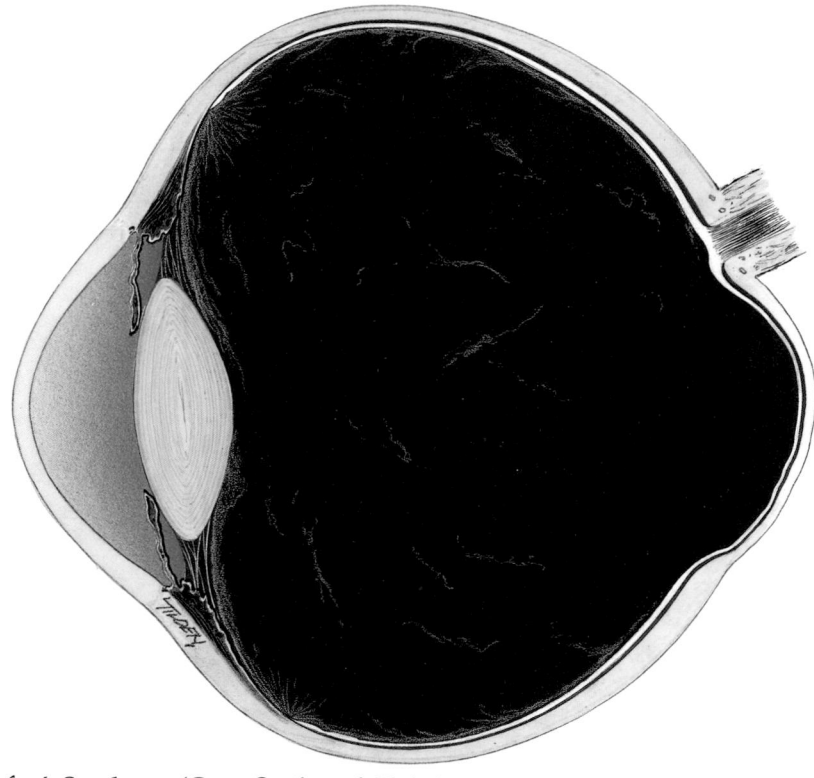

Marfan's Syndrome (Cross Section of Globe)
– Myopia with Posterior Staphyloma

Plate 33   **Homocystinuria**

Homocystinuria

In about 20% of patients with Marfan's syndrome, the metabolic defect involves inadequate homocystine incorporation into tissues, resulting in *homocystinuria* (positive nitroprusside reaction in urine). Patients with homocystinuria (autosomal recessive transmission) are often mentally deficient, whereas patients with Marfan's syndrome have normal intelligence. Also associated with homocystinuria is a tendency for cutaneous flushing and osteoporosis.

Ocular findings in homocystinuria include ectopia lentis, high myopia, lattice degeneration, and an increased tendency to develop peripheral retinal tears and retinal detachments. Removal of a subluxated lens is often accompanied by vitreous loss, which may lead to retinal detachment.

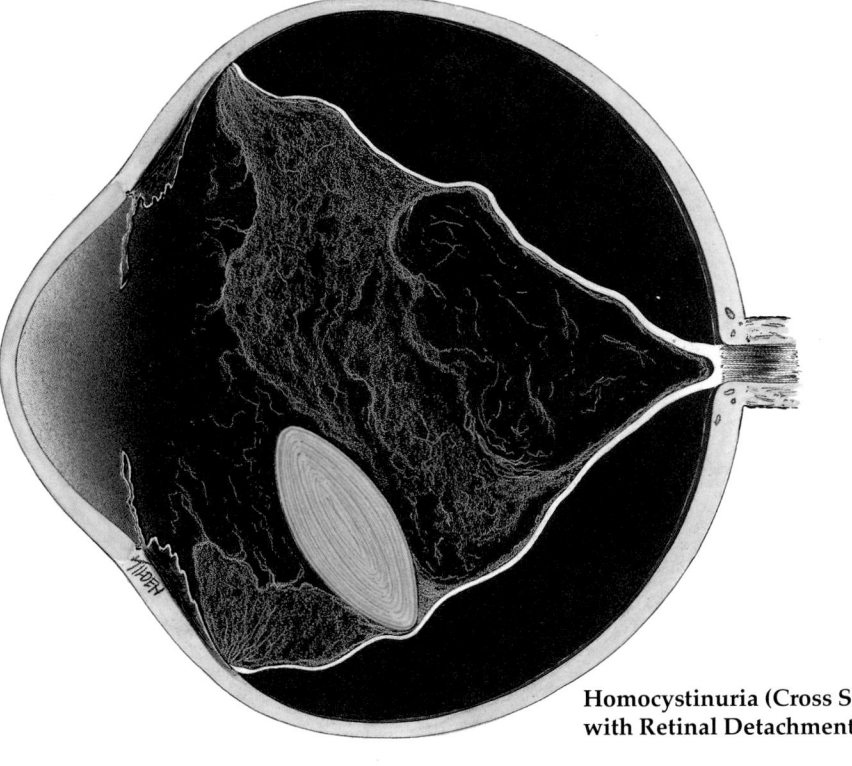

Homocystinuria (Cross Section of Globe) – Dislocated Lens with Retinal Detachment

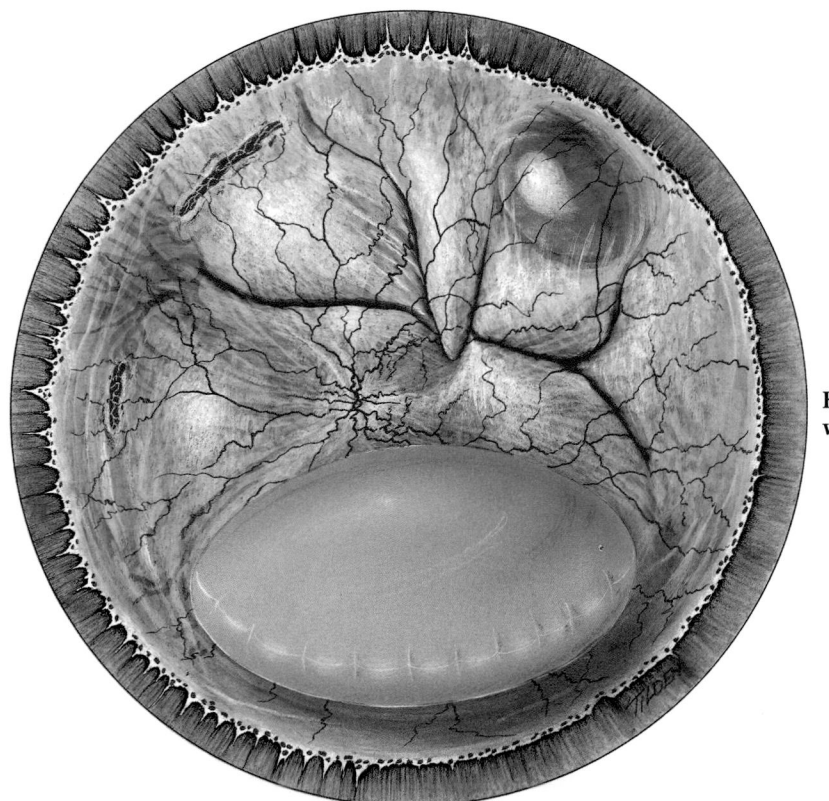

Homocystinuria (Fundus) – Dislocated Lens with Retinal Detachment

Ehlers-Danlos Syndrome

Ehlers-Danlos syndrome is an autosomal dominant inherited biochemical defect involving abnormal formation of collagen fibers. It is manifested clinically in all tissues in which collagen fibers are a main structural component. Hyperelastic and fragile skin, hyperextensibility of the joints especially in the fingers, poor wound healing, and scarring are just some of the manifestations of this connective tissue disorder.

Associated ocular findings in Ehlers-Danlos syndrome include ptosis, hypotony of the extrinsic ocular muscles – often leading to strabismus, Méténier's sign (unusual ease in everting the upper eyelid), epicanthus, myopia, blue sclera, keratoconus, and ectopia lentis.

Vitreoretinal findings in Ehlers-Danlos syndrome include angioid streaks, macular degeneration, equatorial pigmentary degeneration, and retinal breaks (temporal quadrants) with strong vitreoretinal traction forces present. Rolled edges are very often present at the retinal tear sites, along with areas of white-without-pressure. Premature vitreous degeneration (including collapse of the vitreous gel), vitreous hemorrhage, and retinal detachments are associated with Ehlers-Danlos syndrome.

Ehlers-Danlos Syndrome **Plate 34**

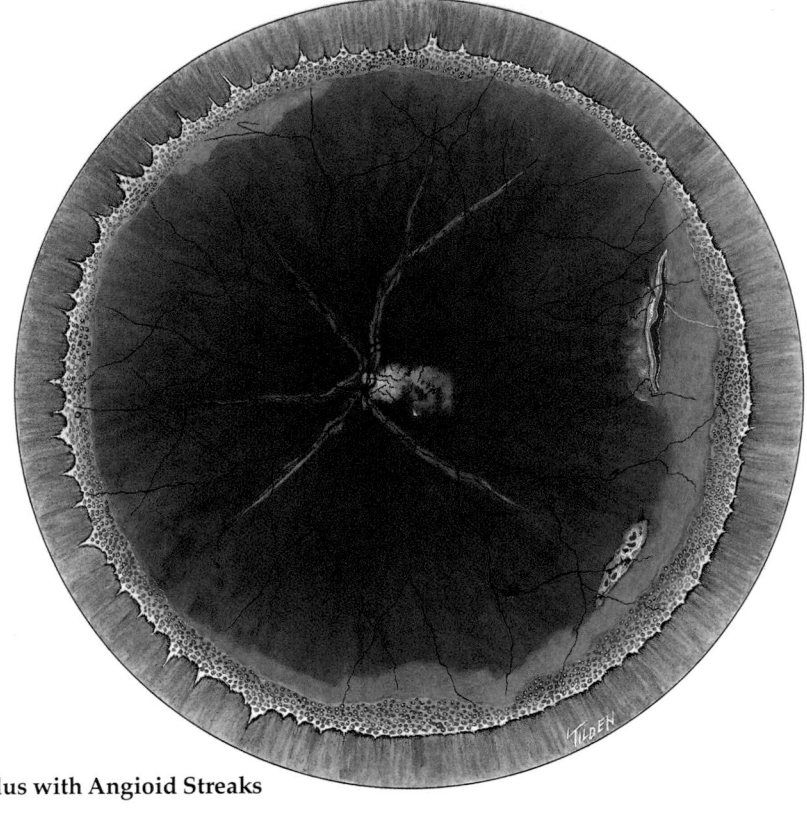

Fundus with Angioid Streaks

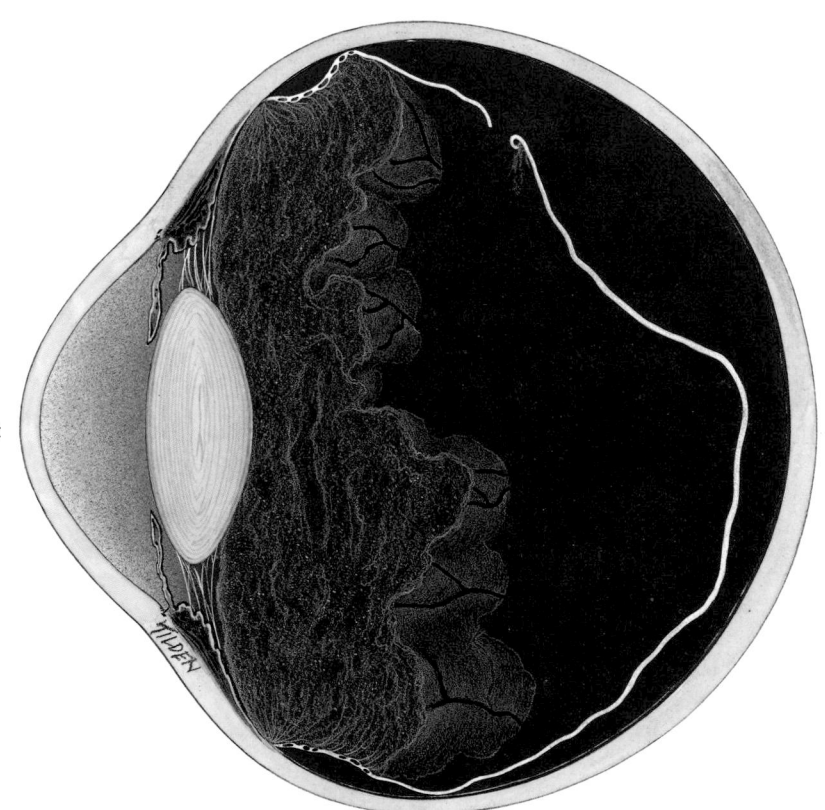

Cross Section of Globe with Retinal Detachment

Degenerative Conditions
of the Vitreous Body

Asteroid Hyalosis
Synchysis Scintillans (Cholesterolosis Oculi)
Amyloidosis of the Vitreous

Plate 35   **Asteroid Hyalosis**

Asteroid Hyalosis

Asteroid hyalosis is characterized by the presence of white spherical particles embedded in the vitreous body. About 27% of patients with asteroid hyalosis are diabetic, yet only 5.4% of diabetic patients have asteroid hyalosis. Therefore, the findings of asteroid hyalosis should alert the examiner to the possibility of diabetes in the patient. Asteroid hyalosis is unilateral in 75% of cases. There is no special sexual or racial predilection. Asteroid hyalosis is usually asymptomatic even in cases where the particles are so numerous that it is difficult to see the retina with indirect ophthalmoscopy. Yet many of the patients do not report decreased visual acuity! The reasons for this discrepancy are not clear.

Biomicroscopically, the yellow-white bodies are characteristically trapped in the anterior and central vitreous gel. They are rarely located in liquefied vitreous, Cloquet's canal, or the retrovitreous space. The asteroid particles are often located along fibrous strands of the vitreous accounting for their "string-of-pearls" appearance. One important feature of the particles in asteroid hyalosis is that, after eye movement, they return to their original position in the vitreous cavity. In contrast, the particles in synchysis scintillans do not return to their original position after eye movements or a change in body position or gravity.

Histopathology studies indicate that asteroid hyalosis bodies are calcium soaps of degenerating vitreous fibers and are associated with a type of foreign body giant cell reaction. The central cores of these particles are birefringent when viewed with polarized light, whereas the capsule or outer portion is not birefringent and appears to be made up of condensed vitreous fibrils. The asteroid particles stain positively with lipid stains (oil red O, Sudan black) and with acid mucopolysaccharide stains (Alcian blue, colloidal iron).

Asteroid hyalosis seldom requires treatment, since it usually is asymptomatic. However, in rare cases it may be responsible for profound visual loss, especially if there is an extremely dense concentration of the particles in the central vitreous cavity. Pars plana vitrectomy can be used to remove the central asteroid bodies and restore vision in these severe cases.

**Cross Section
of Globe**

Synchysis Scintillans (Cholesterolosis Oculi)

Synchysis scintillans is a degenerative condition where cholesterol crystals are deposited in the vitreous, in the anterior chamber, and in the subretinal space. This is a relatively rare condition, but it is usually secondary to ocular trauma, chronic recurrent intraocular hemorrhage, or inflammation.

Patients usually do not complain of visual symptoms from the vitreous opacities because the vision is extremely poor in that eye, either from a retinal detachment or a cataract. If iridocyclitis or glaucoma occurs as a result of cholesterolosis of the anterior chamber (resembles a hypopyon), then the patient may experience ocular pain.

Ophthalmoscopy reveals numerous multicolored glittering crystalline particles whose size and shape are quite variable. With ocular movement they are dispersed and resemble multicolored confetti and then settle by gravity when eye movement stops. Biomicroscopy shows extensive liquefaction of the vitreous in synchysis scintillans. The particles are flat with angular edges and are multicolored.

Microscopic examination indicates that most of the crystals are cholesterol, although tyrosine, leucine, and margarine crystals have also been found. The origin of the crystalline particles in synchysis scintillans remains obscure. One hypothesis suggests that a cholesterol-fatty acid-ester combination in the blood is the source. Once inside the eye, the molecule breaks down, releasing free cholesterol and fatty acids. Since free cholesterol is highly insoluble, it crystallizes out of solution. Another theory suggests that the crystalline particles may originate from a lens that is ruptured secondary to trauma. As for treatment, patients with synchysis scintillans usually do not require treatment unless the particles clog the aqueous drainage system, resulting in glaucoma. In such cases, the particles are irrigated from the anterior chamber.

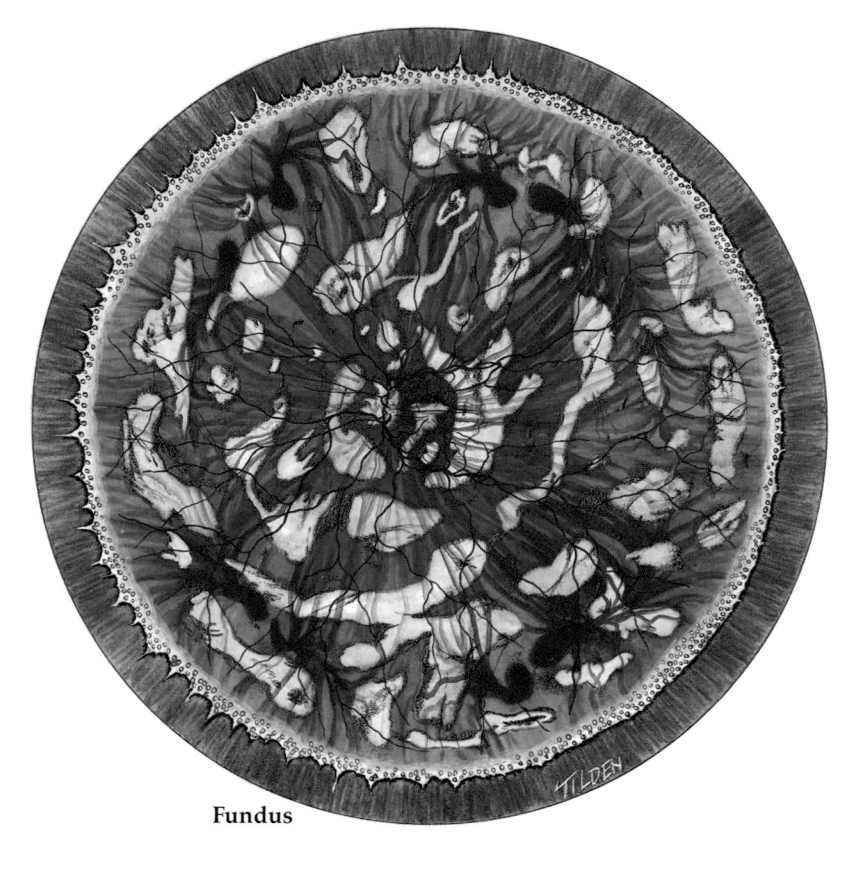

Fundus

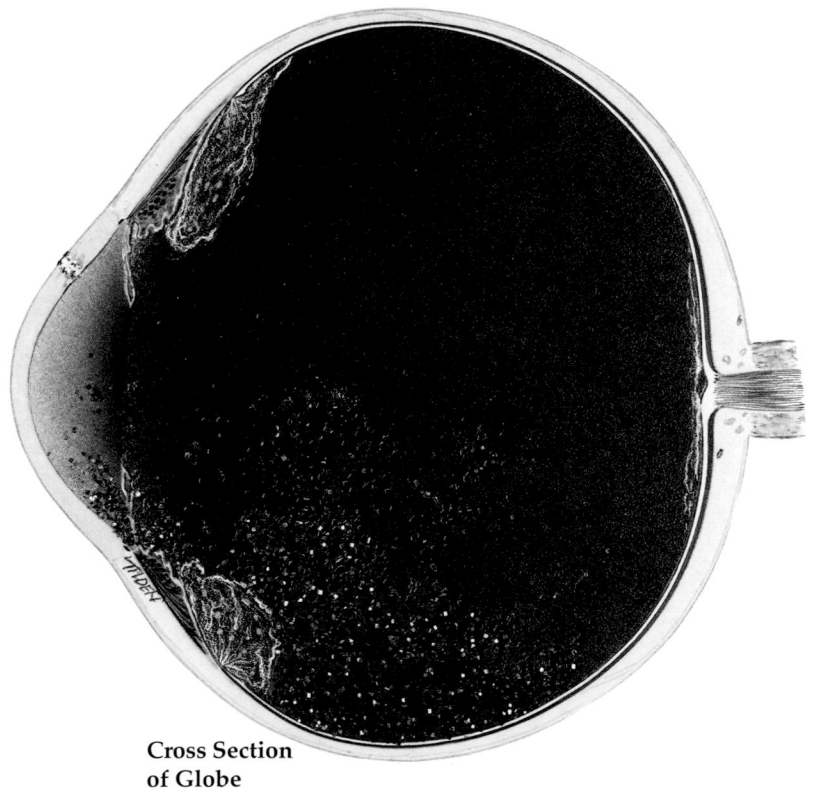

**Cross Section
of Globe**

Amyloidosis of the Vitreous

Primary amyloidosis involves the deposition of amyloid material along collagen fibers and usually involves the heart, pancreas, thyroid, eye, peripheral nerves, and muscles and is not associated with debilitating diseases. *Secondary amyloidosis* involves the deposition of amyloid material along reticulin fibers and usually involves the liver, spleen, adrenal glands, and kidney and is associated with chronic debilitating diseases such as neoplasms, metabolic disorders, infectious and noninfectious chronic inflammations, and dysproteinemias.

Primary heredofamilial amyloidosis involves ocular tissues and is transmitted as a simple Mendelian dominant trait. Elevations of the β_1- and α_2-lipoprotein fractions seem to suggest that an anomaly of lipoprotein metabolism may be present in primary amyloidosis.

Systemic manifestations of primary amyloidosis include weight loss, generalized weakness, and progressive peripheral neuropathy, as well as cardiovascular, gastrointestinal, and endocrine disorders. Symptoms appear usually by the second decade.

Ocular involvement is found in 8% of patients with primary amyloidosis and can be manifested by photophobia, sudden loss of vision, diplopia, blepharospasm, external ophthalmoplegia, and sluggish pupils, as well as "cotton-wool" retinal exudates and vitreous opacities (see Table 7.1).

Early ophthalmoscopic changes seen in the fundus consist of a whitish lesion in the wall of a retinal arteriole, which develops cottonlike fringes in the vitreous cortex. Then the paravascular "cotton-wool" spot spreads out and grows into the vitreous cavity. As the opacities become denser, they obscure the underlying retinal architecture. Amyloid deposits can cover the disc and macular region and be responsible for a marked decrease in central vision. The affected vitreous gel has a "glass-wool" appearance to it. When a posterior vitreous detachment takes place, the amyloid deposits may detach from the retinal surface and shift position. Sometimes these amyloid deposits become displaced along the visual axis, thereby reducing vision.

The differential diagnosis of these amyloid vitreous opacities should include inflammatory vitreous exudates from chorioretinitic foci or pars planitis. Usually there are chorioretinal foci that identify the source of the vitreous exudate. Pars planitis has exudates in the pars plana as well as in the vitreous, whereas amyloidosis does not have a pars plana "exudate." Other differential diagnostic possibilities include an organized vitreous hemorrhage, which, if old, has a membranous, dirty white-yellow appearance. Usually, there are some unresolved red blood clots, and with time these tend to melt away or clear partially, whereas amyloidosis is relentlessly progressive. Retained intraocular metallic foreign bodies and parasitic foreign bodies have a membranous quality to them, often with a hemorrhagic element, which is not characteristic of amyloidosis.

Table 7.1. Primary Heredofamilial Amyloidosis

Ocular symptoms
    Diplopia
    Photophobia
    Progressive loss of vision
    Sudden loss of vision

Ocular signs
    Blepharospasm
    Bilateral exophthalmos
    External ophthalmoplegia
    Anisocoria
    Sluggish pupillary reflexes
    Retinal hemorrhages
    Paravascular retinal exudates (amyloid)
        "Cotton-wool" exudates
    Blood vessel wall deposits (amyloid)
        Central retinal artery
        Short posterior ciliary vessels
    Vitreous changes
        Both eyes affected
        Vitreous opacities ("glass-wool")

Amyloidosis of the Vitreous   **Plate 37**

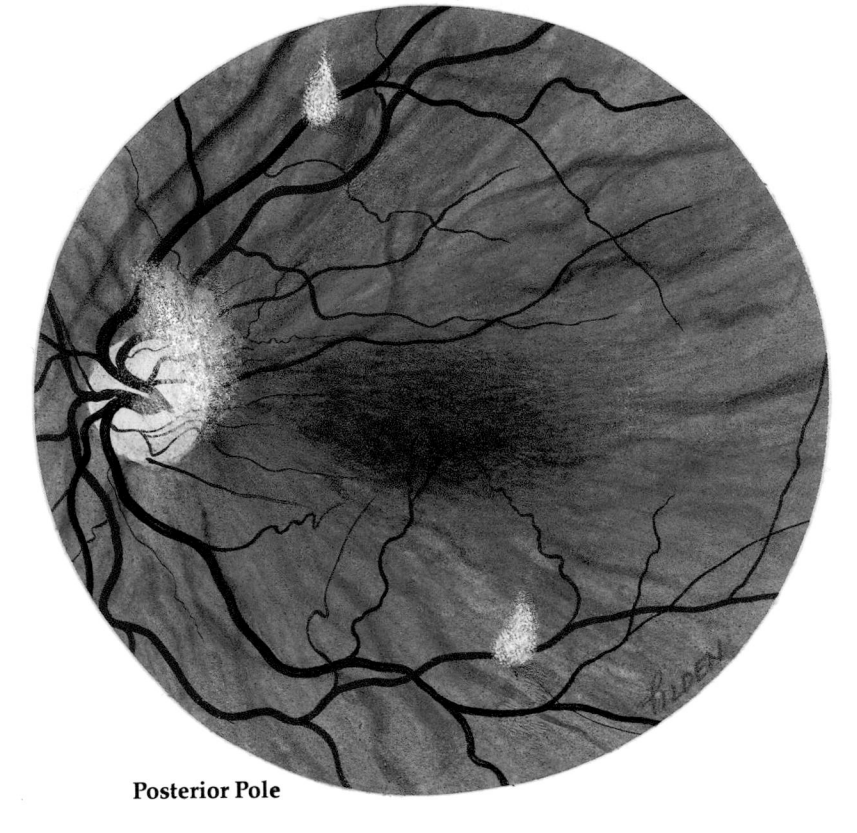

Posterior Pole

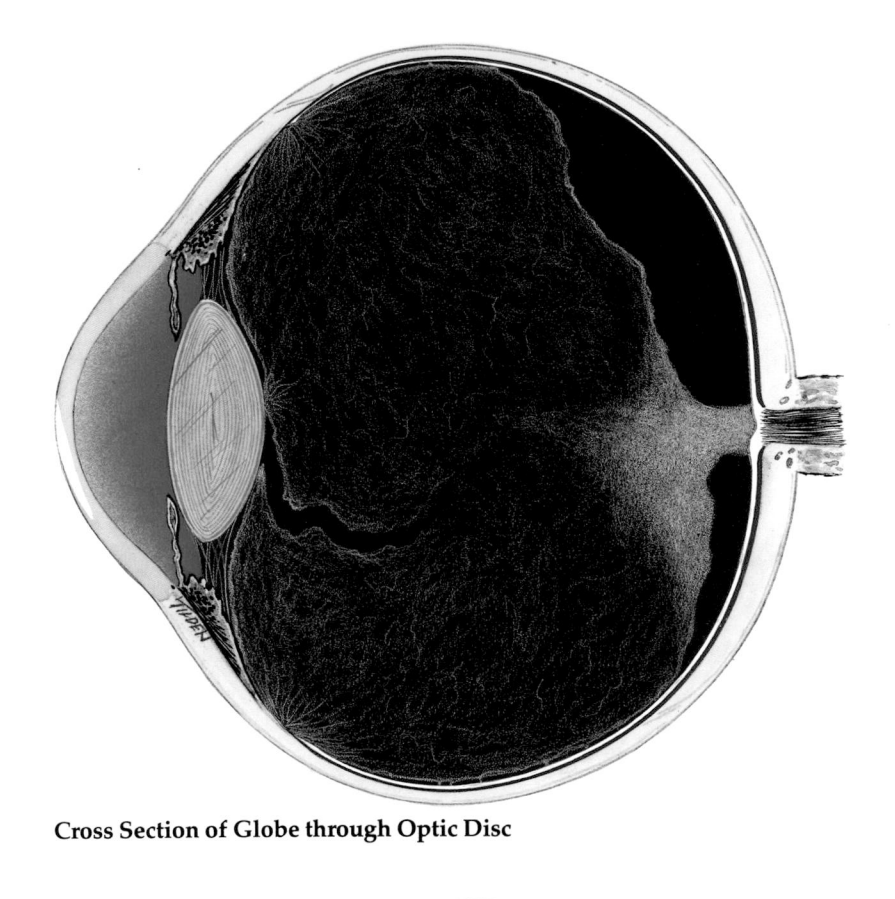

Cross Section of Globe through Optic Disc

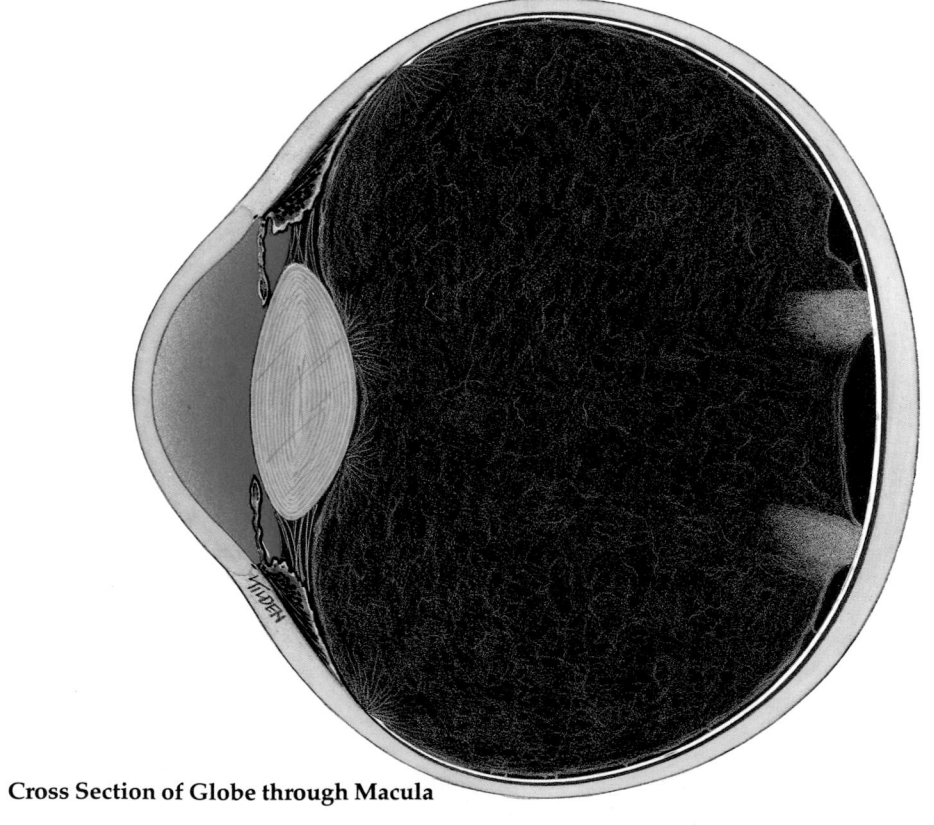

Cross Section of Globe through Macula

Proliferative Retinopathies 8

Diabetic Retinopathy
   Background Diabetic Retinopathy
   Preproliferative Diabetic Retinopathy
   Proliferative Diabetic Retinopathy

Retinal Vein Occlusion
Sickle Cell Retinopathy
Retrolental Fibroplasia

Diabetic Retinopathy

Diabetes mellitus is a genetically determined metabolic disorder characterized clinically by elevated fasting blood sugars, arteriosclerotic and microangiopathic vasculopathies and neuropathies. The exact pathogenic sequence of diabetic retinopathy has yet to be worked out, but it appears that the elevated blood sugars and decreased plasma insulin levels influence the pituitary gland to manufacture and release increased amounts of human growth hormone into the plasma. The increased growth hormone potentiates hepatic protein synthesis of α_2-globulins and fibrinogen. These macromolecules act as electrostatic bridges between neighboring red blood cells and platelets resulting in abnormal red blood cells as well as platelet aggregates. These abnormal aggregates clog up capillary channels leading to downstream hypoxia and, in some cases, ischemia. Microaneurysms (aborted attempts at neovascularization) and actual retinal and/or optic disc neovascularization may develop in an effort to correct the hypoxia problems in the retinal tissues.

The overall incidence of diabetes mellitus involves about 5% of the general population. Of all known diabetics, 8% are less than 25 years of age when the diagnosis is made; 22% are diagnosed between the ages of 25 and 44 years, and 50% are diagnosed between the ages of 45 and 64 years of age; 20% of diabetics are diagnosed after 65 years of age. Approximately 50% of all diabetics will have some form of retinopathy at the time that their diabetes is diagnosed, and it is related to age of onset and duration of the diabetes mellitus. The overall incidence of proliferative diabetic retinopathy is 4.4% of all diabetics. Surprisingly, there is a higher incidence of proliferative diabetic retinopathy among non-insulin-dependent diabetics than among insulin-dependent diabetics.

Diabetic retinopathy can be divided into three separate stages: (1) background (nonproliferative) retinopathy, (2) preproliferative retinopathy, and (3) proliferative retinopathy.

Background Diabetic Retinopathy
Background diabetic retinopathy is characterized by an initial dilation in the retinal veins, retinal microaneurysms, dot-blot or deep round retinal hemorrhages, and/or deep hard waxy retinal exudates. Microaneurysms and retinal vessels may leak, producing localized or diffuse retinal edema, including macular edema with concomitant visual loss. Background diabetic retinopathy predominantly affects the posterior pole.

Preproliferative Diabetic Retinopathy
The preproliferative stage of diabetic retinopathy usually consists of cotton-wool spots in addition to the background diabetic retinopathy changes already described. The cotton-wool spot represents hypoxia and/or ischemia in the inner surface of the retina at the nerve fiber layer. Eventually, there is resolution or clearing of the cotton-wool spot, but often at the edge of the cotton-wool spot, neovascularization of the retina may develop. For these reasons, the cotton-wool spot stage (unrelated to systemic hypertension) in a diabetic is referred to as the preproliferative stage. In addition, retinal venous beading and intraretinal microvascular abnormalities (IRMA), which refer to dilated retinal capillary shunt vessels around areas of capillary bed nonperfusion (fluorescein angiographic finding) may also be present.

Proliferative Diabetic Retinopathy
In the proliferative stage, retinal and/or disc neovascularization has taken place in addition to the preproliferative retinopathy findings already present. The new blood vessels grow and may progress to a point where there is connective tissue or glial proliferation that accompanies the neovascularization process. The new vessels may grow into and become adherent to the vitreous body. In some cases, there is spontaneous regression of the neovascularization network with contracture of the connective tissue components, and this may lead to secondary vitreous hemorrhage, vitreous membranes, and a traction or a rhegmatogenous retinal detachment. These reactions may still take place without any regression of the neovascularization and connective tissue networks. Repeated vitreous hemorrhages can lead to more vitreoretinal membranes with further traction and vitreous hemorrhage in a vicious cycle (retinitis proliferans) leading to total retinal detachment, blindness and phthisis bulbi.

Leaking retinal microaneurysms in the macular region have been treated with either focal or grid pattern argon laser photocoagulation to control macular edema and stabilize vision. Pan retinal argon laser photocoagulation has been successful in controlling proliferative diabetic retinopathy and reducing the chances of intraocular hemorrhage in early cases. Pars plana vitrectomy and scleral buckling surgery have helped restore vision in advanced cases of proliferative diabetic retinopathy with nonresolving vitreous hemorrhages and with tractional retinal detachments.

Diabetic Retinopathy **Plate 38**

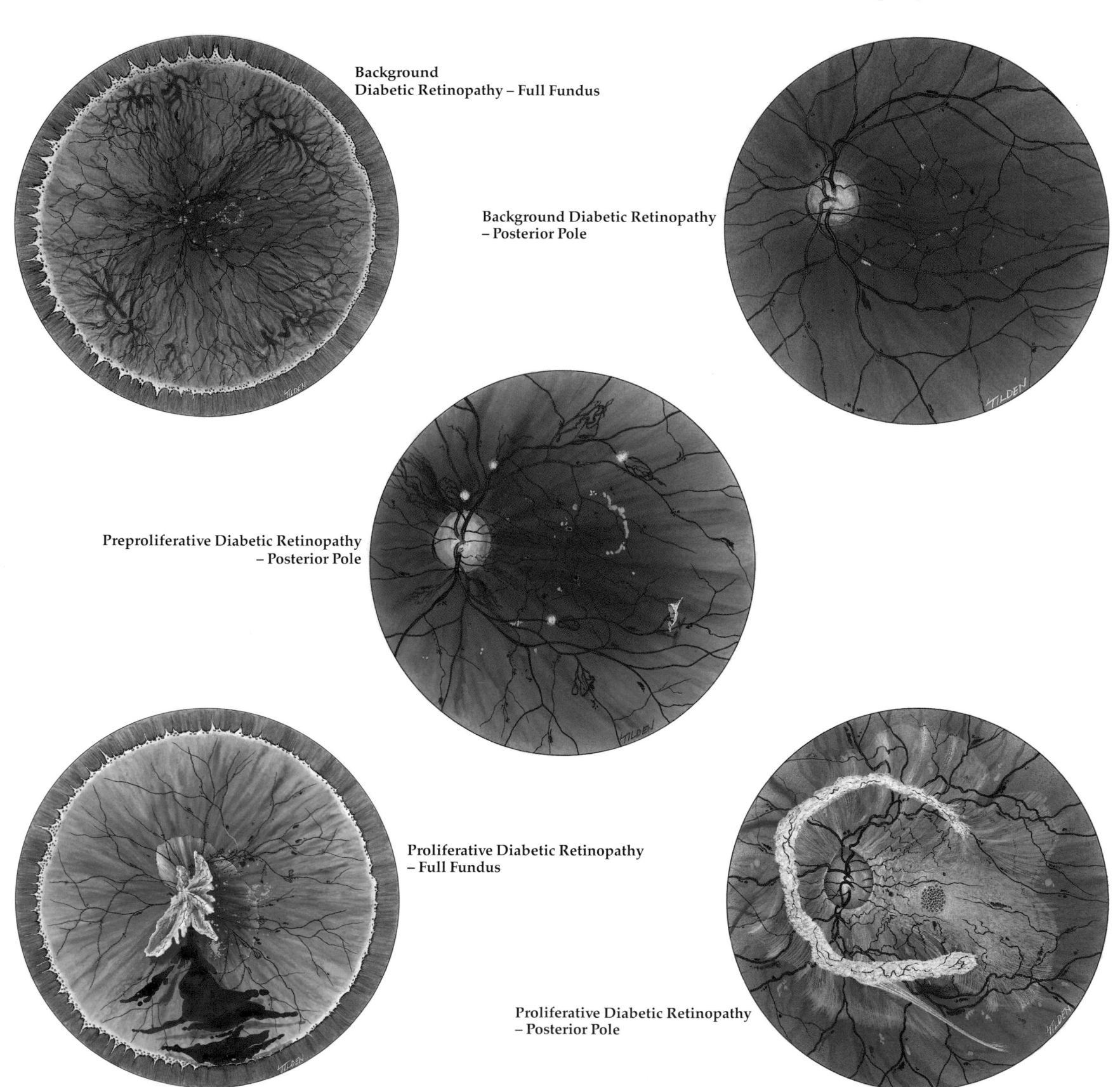

Background
Diabetic Retinopathy – Full Fundus

Background Diabetic Retinopathy
– Posterior Pole

Preproliferative Diabetic Retinopathy
– Posterior Pole

Proliferative Diabetic Retinopathy
– Full Fundus

Proliferative Diabetic Retinopathy
– Posterior Pole

Retinal Vein Occlusion

Retinal vein occlusions are usually due to arteriosclerosis and systemic hypertension. Among branch retinal vein occlusions, the superotemporal branch (63%) is more commonly affected than the inferotemporal branch retinal vein (38%). This increased incidence of the superotemporal branch retinal vein occluding correlates with its larger number of arteriovenous crossings (3) compared to the arteriovenous crossings (2) in the other quadrants.

Characteristically, an acute branch retinal vein occlusion has superficial splinter retinal hemorrhages, deep round retinal hemorrhages, as well as widened and more tortuous retinal veins in the sector of the obstruction. Retinal edema, including macular edema (58%) with concomitant reduction in visual acuity, is often present. On occasion, cotton-wool spots may also be noted as well as retinal microaneurysms. Other adverse macular sequelae include macular hole formation, surface wrinkling retinopathy, granularity and/or hyperpigmentation of the retinal pigment epithelium, macular exudates, detachments, and hemorrhage. In the later stages, intraretinal neovascularization (73%), preretinal neovascularization (23%), and secondary vitreous hemorrhage (20%) may develop, which, in turn, could lead to vitreoretinal membranes and a possible traction and/or rhegmatogenous retinal detachment. Eyes with retinal vein occlusions that have wide areas of capillary bed nonperfusion are more likely to develop retinal and/or optic disc neovascularization. Eyes with central retinal vein occlusions are more likely to develop neovascularization than those with branch retinal vein occlusions. Also, patients who develop optic disc and/or retinal neovascularization may go on to acquire rubeosis iridis with hemorrhagic glaucoma. Aphakic eyes are more prone to this complication than phakic eyes. Compensatory vascular reactions to the vein occlusion involve the development of various collaterals, for example, vein to vein.

Retinal Vein Occlusion **Plate 39**

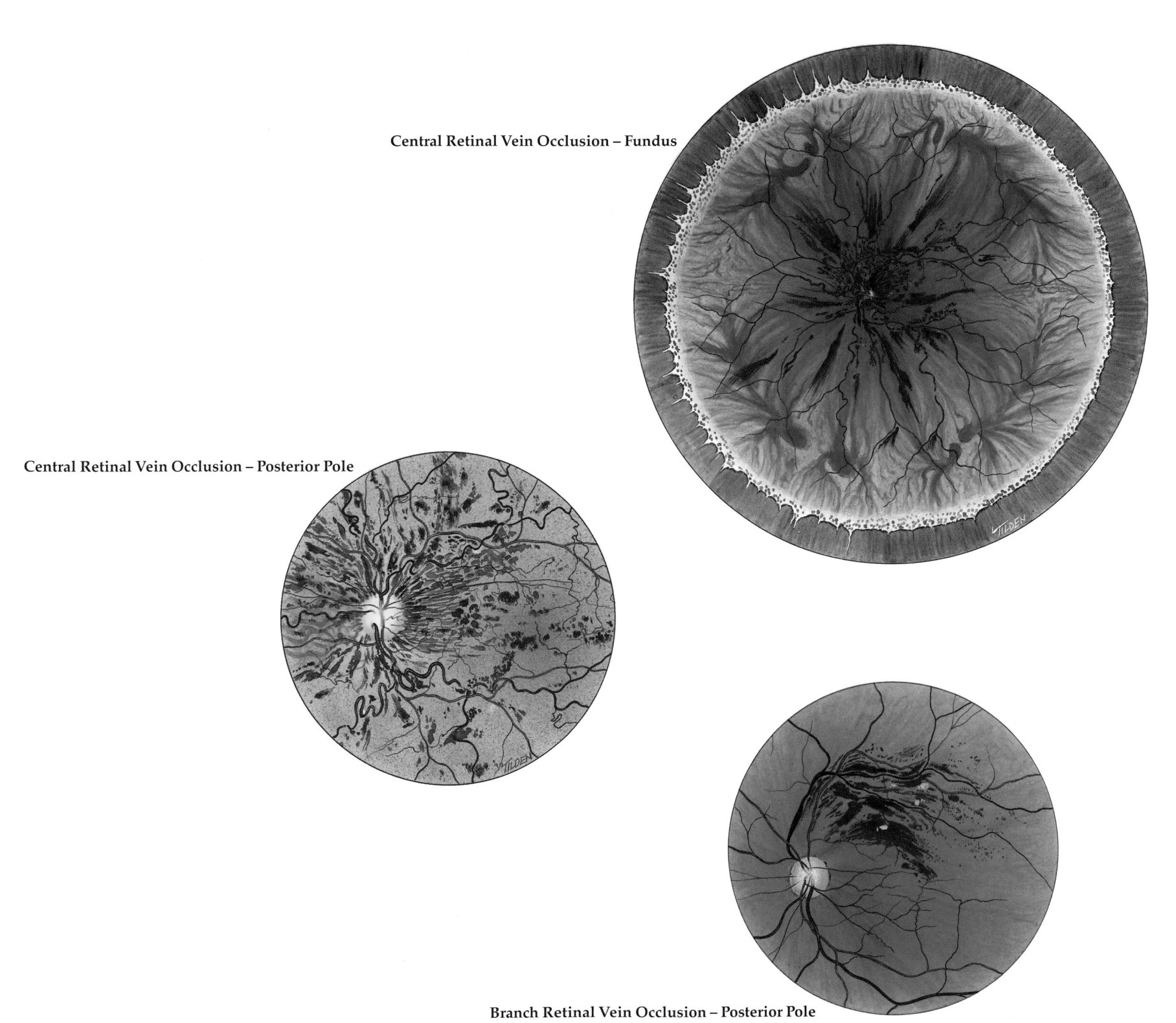

Central Retinal Vein Occlusion – Fundus

Central Retinal Vein Occlusion – Posterior Pole

Branch Retinal Vein Occlusion – Posterior Pole

Sickle Cell Retinopathy

Hemoglobin S has the tendency to become insoluble and turn to a gel when deoxygenated, leading to highly abnormal viscous aggregates of sickled (crescent-shaped) red blood cells, which, in turn, may cause vascular obstruction. The abnormal hemoglobins in this family include SS, SC, and AS.

Ophthalmoscopically, sickle cell retinopathy usually presents with dilated tortuous retinal veins, and discoid-shaped retinal scars, which have been termed the "black sunburst" sign. Patients with Hb-SC disease have characteristic equatorial arteriovenous vascular shunts projecting into the vitreous termed "sea fans." Vitreous hemorrhages often accompany patients with sea fans, and this can go on to the formation of vitreoretinal membranes with traction and/or rhegmatogenous retinal detachments. Sickle cell patients with hemoglobin SC retinopathy have been divided by Goldberg (1971) into five separate clinical stages, which, in some cases, are progressive (Table 8.1).

Table 8.1.

Proliferative Sickle Cell (Hb-SC) Retinopathy

Stage	Features
I	Peripheral arteriolar occlusions
II	Peripheral arteriolar-venular anastamoses (sea fans)
III	Neovascular and fibrous proliferations
IV	Vitreous hemorrhage
V	Retinal detachment

Reprinted with permission from Goldberg MF: Classification and pathogenesis of proliferative sickle retinopathy. Ophthalmology 71: 649–665. Philadelphia, Lippincott/Harper & Row, 1971

Proliferative Sickle Cell Retinopathy   **Plate 40**

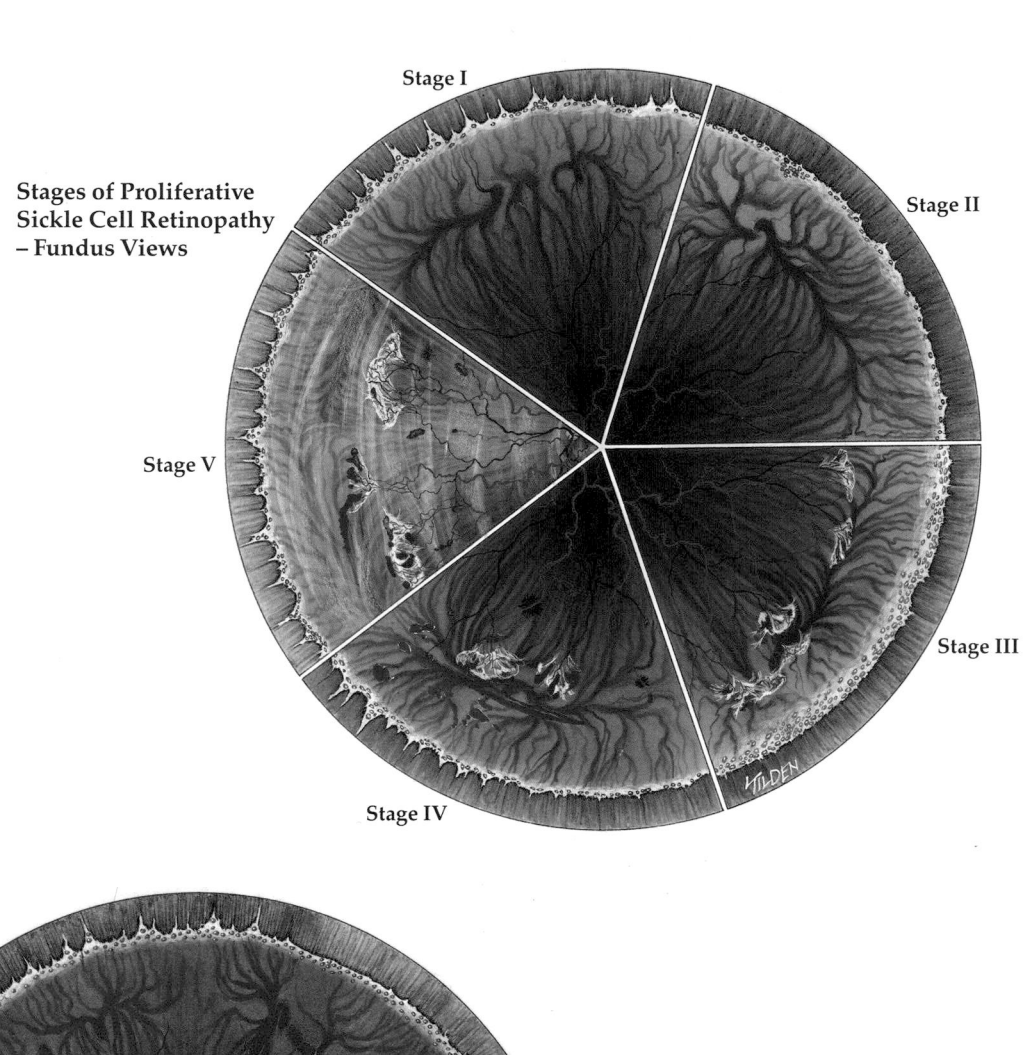

**Stages of Proliferative
Sickle Cell Retinopathy
– Fundus Views**

Stage I

Stage II

Stage III

Stage IV

Stage V

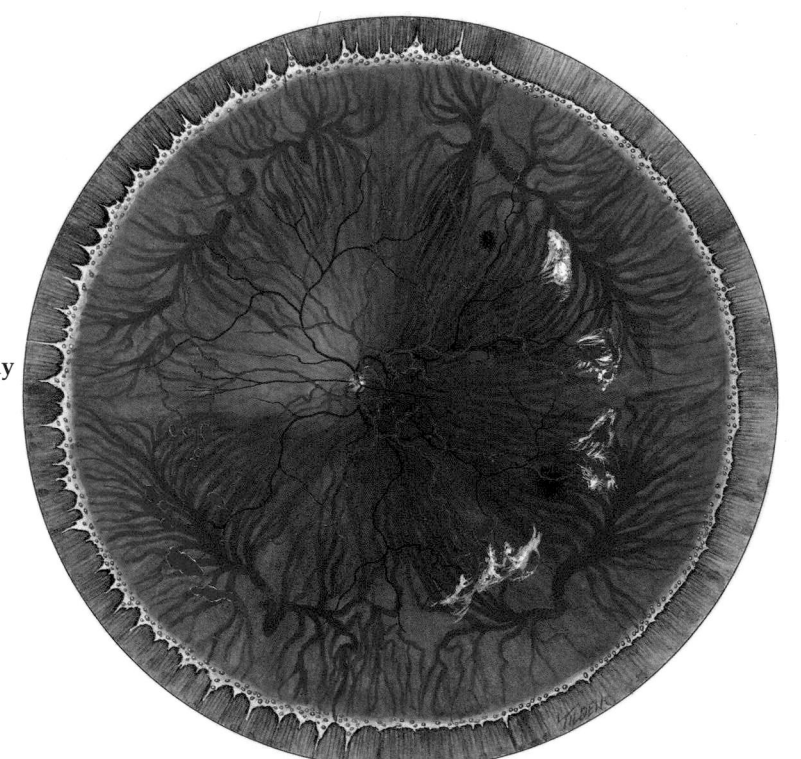

**Proliferative Sickle Cell Retinopathy
– Stage IV (Fundus)**

Retrolental Fibroplasia

Retrolental fibroplasia (RLF) is usually seen when premature infants are treated with "too much oxygen" for respiratory distress. Rarely does RLF occur in full-term infants that are given oxygen therapy. The reasons for this are that premature infants do not have a completely developed or mature retinal vasculature in the retinal periphery, especially in the temporal quadrants compared to the nasal quadrants. The immature retinal vasculature is susceptible to the effects of high concentrations of oxygen, which provoke an initial vasoconstriction followed by retinal neovascularization and the development of RLF. In full-term infants, the retinal vasculature is "mature" and does not undergo the proliferative reactions in the presence of elevated concentrations of oxygen.

The development of retinal vessels begins at the optic disc at about the fourth month of gestation and reaches the ora serrata by the eighth month of gestation. The distance from the optic nerve head to the ora serrata in the temporal quadrants is greater than the distance from the optic disc to the ora serrata in the nasal quadrants. There is greater immaturity of the temporal retinal periphery than the nasal retinal periphery during the gestational period, which may be the reason that in premature infants treated with excessive oxygen there is a predilection for RLF to be found in temporal quadrants as opposed to nasal quadrants.

The precise mechanism by which oxygen leads to vaso-obliteration of the immature retinal capillaries is not known. However, it is believed that high oxygen concentrations are toxic to actively growing capillary endothelial cells, which leads, in some way, to obliteration of the developing capillary bed. Once obliteration occurs, proliferative neovascular tissues develop, leading to acute retrolental fibroplasia. In some cases there is spontaneous regression, in others, a cicatricial phase follows with varying amounts of tissue damage, including vitreoretinal membranes, exudative, traction, and/or rhegmatogenous retinal detachments. Retrolental fibroplasia eyes also have a characteristic high myopia, congenital nystagmus, amblyopia, and strabismus. The various stages of retrolental fibroplasia are listed in Table 8.2.

Table 8.2.

Stages of Retrolental Fibroplasia

Stage	Ocular Findings
Acute Phase	Vaso-obliterative (while on O_2) Vasoproliferative (after O_2 is discontinued) Large arteriovenous shunt + proliferative capillaries Spontaneous regression (80 %)
Chronic Phase (Cicatricial 20 %)[1]	
Grade I	Myopia Retinal pigmentation Vitreous membranes Equatorial retinal folds

Grade II	Grade I plus:
	   Dragging of the retina
	   Ectopic macula
	   Neovascularization
	   Elevated retinal vessels
	   Lattice degeneration
	   Retinal breaks

Grade III	Falciform retinal folds Amblyopia Ocular nystagmus
Grade IV	Rhegmatogenous retinal detachment Tractional exudative retinal detachment
Grade V	Organized retinal detachment

[1] Reprinted with permission from Tasman W: Late complications of retrolental fibroplasia. Ophthalmology 86 (10): 1724–40. Philadelphia, Lippincott/Harper & Row, 1979

Retrolental Fibroplasia   Plate 41

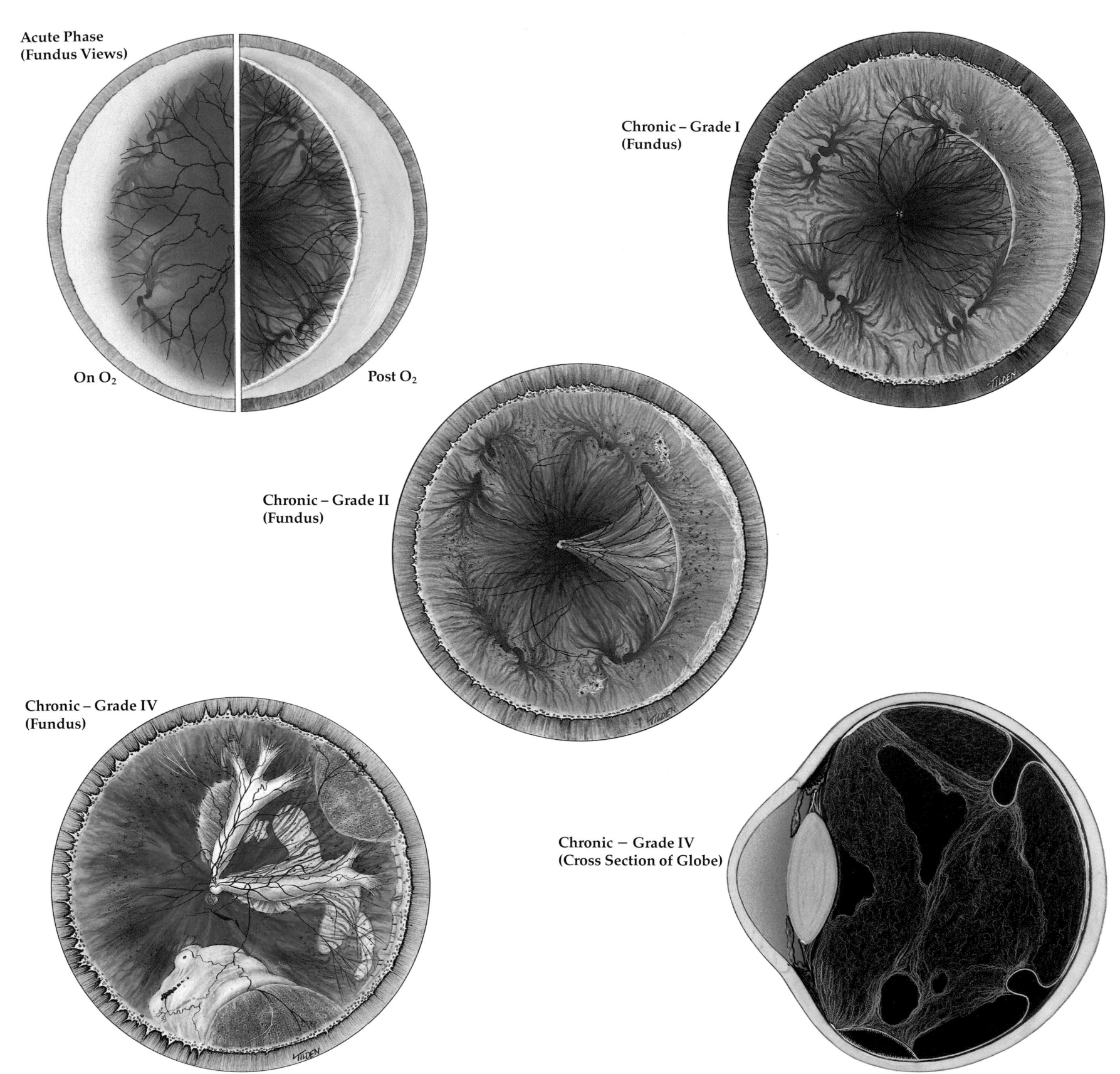

Acute Phase (Fundus Views)

On O₂

Post O₂

Chronic – Grade I (Fundus)

Chronic – Grade II (Fundus)

Chronic – Grade IV (Fundus)

Chronic – Grade IV (Cross Section of Globe)

Inflammatory Disorders 9

Plate 42   **Sarcoidosis**

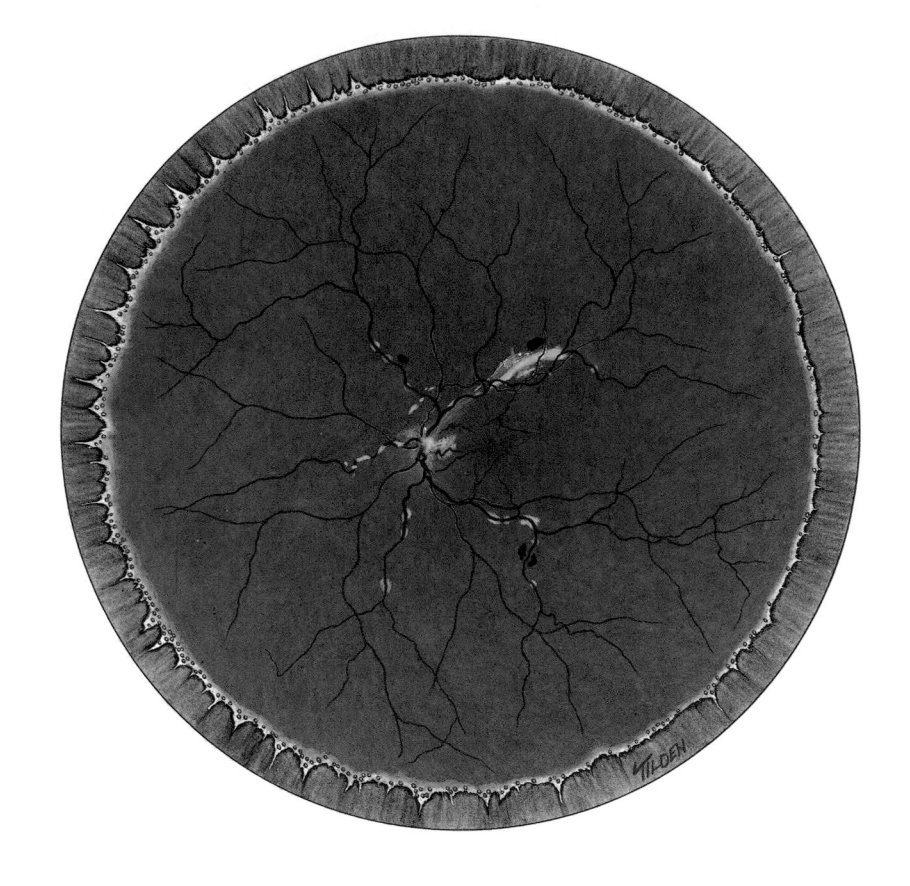

Sarcoidosis

Sarcoidosis is an inflammatory disorder of unknown origin more common in blacks than in whites and is characterized by fever, arthritis, lymphadenopathy, central nervous system as well as ocular lesions. The basic lesion consists of a focal noncaseating granuloma containing nodular collections of epithelioid cells.

Ocular manifestations of sarcoidosis include conjunctival nodules, a granulomatous uveitis (anterior and/or posterior), and retinal as well as optic nerve involvement. A retinal periphlebitis along with retinal hemorrhages, vitreous veils, and intraretinal and subretinal pigment epithelium granulomas may be present. There is a perivascular collection of lymphocytes along the retinal veins, which have periphlebitis. Intense retinal periphlebitis, in sarcoidosis, may produce the typical appearance of "candle-wax drippings" which have a predilection for the retinal veins within the posterior pole. Small superficial retinal hemorrhages may also be noted. In some cases, there is diffuse choroidal involvement leading to focal pigmentary atrophy and scarring.

Sarcoidosis that involves the central nervous system may also affect the optic nerve producing a picture of papillitis and papilledema.

Harada's Syndrome
(Vogt-Koyanagi-Harada Syndrome)

Harada's syndrome is an inflammatory disorder of un-known etiology that affects young adult blacks, orientals, and darkly pigmented Caucasians. There is no particular sexual predilection, with males and females equally af-fected. Patients may present with headaches, nausea, tin-nitus, and general malaise. Meningeal irritation can be re-sponsible for cerebrospinal pleocytosis and a stiff neck. In the later stages of the disease, poliosis and alopecia are seen.

Ocular findings consist of a bilateral granulomatous uveitis, ocular pain, redness, and photophobia, with a number of inflammatory cells found in the aqueous and vit-reous. There are often multiple dome-shaped exudative de-tachments of the neurosensory retina. There is retinal edema, and, on occasion, some retinal hemorrhages may be present. The shifting subretinal fluid may be clear or turbid. In some cases, the multiple retinal detachment sites coalesce into a large retinal detachment due to the effects of gravity. Typically, no retinal tears are present. The source of the sub-retinal fluid is not well established, but histopathologic analysis of eyes with Harada's syndrome reveals a diffuse granulomatous uveitis involving the choriocapillaris similar to that of sympathetic uveitis.

Some patients with Harada's syndrome respond to sys-temic steroids. In others, a spontaneous resolution of the in-flammatory process takes place with reattachment of the re-tina, leaving focal areas of retinal pigmentary atrophy.

Plate 44   **Pars Planitis**

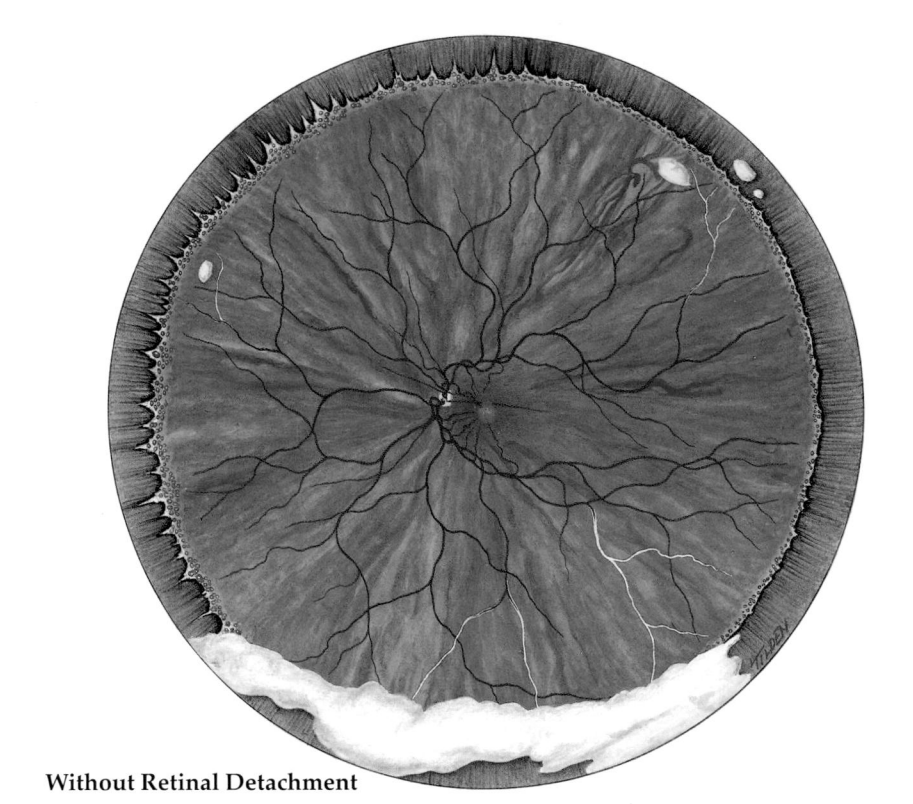

Without Retinal Detachment

With Retinal Detachment

Pars Planitis (Idiopathic Peripheral Uveoretinitis)

Pars planitis is a chronic inflammatory process of unknown etiology affecting the peripheral fundus (retina and choroid) and the ciliary body. It tends to occur at any age, but is most severe in children and young adults. There is no particular sexual predilection with males and females equally affected by the disease. The disease is bilateral in 95% of cases and is thought by some investigators to involve a special hypersensitivity reaction to the small retinal vessels in the fundus periphery.

Ocular findings in idiopathic peripheral uveoretinitis in clude decreased visual acuity, normotensive or hypotensive globes, and aqueous flare with several nongranulomatous keratic precipitates, along with inflammatory cells in the anterior vitreous. White exudates (snow banks) are noted mostly inferiorly in the region of the pars plana and the vitreous base. The peripheral retinal veins appear dilated, and on occasion have perivascular infiltrates. There is often cystoid macular edema in the more severe cases.

Pars planitis tends to be a chronic condition with remissions and exacerbations. However, there is a smoldering inflammation, which leads to adverse sequelae, for example, peripheral anterior synechiae, posterior subcapsular cataracts, organization of the vitreous with vitreoretinal membranes, and traction on peripheral retinal tissues, leading to traction and/or rhegmatogenous retinal detachments and, in some cases, retinoschisis. In addition, glaucoma, band keratopathy, and dense cataracts may lead to further visual loss and blindness.

Choroidal Detachments (Ciliochoroidal Effusion)

Choroidal Detachment   **Plate 45**

Choroidal detachments represent an accumulation of fluid within the suprachoroidal space (outermost layer of the choroid) and the supraciliaris space (outermost layer of the ciliary body). Although there is a detachment of the uveal tract from the inner layer of the sclera, choroidal detachments actually represent fluid accumulation within the uveal tract.

Characteristically, choroidal detachments have a brown-orange coloration, are solid-appearing elevations under intact retinal pigment epithelium and choroidal tissue layers. Choroidal detachments do not undulate with ocular movements like rhegmatogenous retinal detachments, and they do not shift under gravitational influences as do exudative retinal detachments of the neurosensory retina.

Most choroidal detachments contain serous fluid, but some are due to a choroidal hemorrhage. On occasion, a solid choroidal detachment containing tumor tissue, for example, melanoma, may be present, but ultrasonography usually can clear up the nature (solid, serous, or hemorrhagic) of the choroidal detachment.

Choroidal detachments are often due to ocular surgery or trauma to the globe where inflammation and/or hypotony are created initially, and then choroidal detachments develop secondarily. In the other cases, there is an initial rhegmatogenous retinal detachment that creates ocular hypotony, which in turn leads to the development of choroidal detachments. Once the ciliary body detaches, aqueous humor production is reduced, leading to more hypotony, which in turn leads to increased choroidal detachments. Retinal detachments that have choroidal detachments present usually have a greater chance of developing proliferative vitreoretinopathy (massive periretinal proliferation), and, in general, have a poorer visual prognosis than rhegmatogenous retinal detachments that do not have associated choroidal detachments.

Plate 46   **Choroidal Effusion Syndrome**

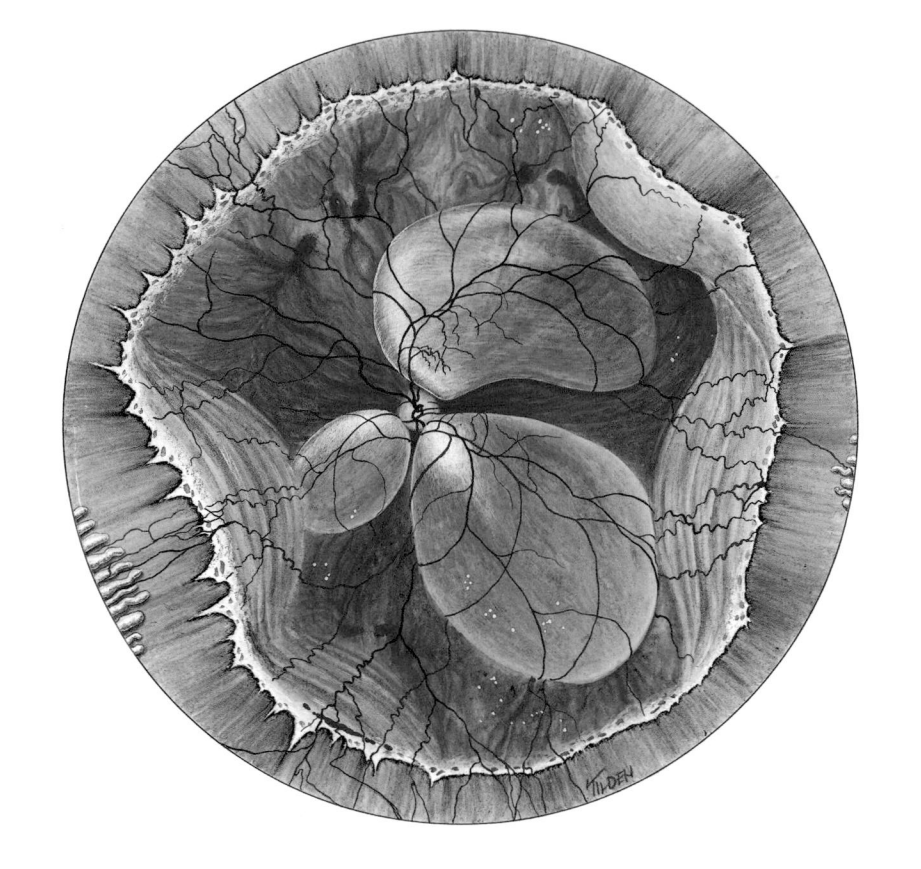

Choroidal Effusion Syndrome

The choroidal effusion syndrome is characterized by non-rhegmatogenous retinal detachment with shifting subretinal fluid, choroidal detachments, and an associated increased protein content in the cerebrospinal fluid. The patients are usually in their fifth or sixth decades of life and males and females are equally affected. The patients respond to systemic steroids, but do very poorly with scleral buckling surgery.

The differential diagnosis of the choroidal effusion syndrome detachments includes the following conditions: rhegmatogenous retinal detachments, choroidal tumors, metastatic tumors to the choroid, choroidal hemangiomas, vitreous hemorrhage, and subretinal pigment epithelial hemorrhage, and reactive lymphoid hyperplasia of the uveal tract.

Pigmentary Tumors of the Peripheral Retina

10

Choroidal Nevi
Congenital Hypertrophy of the Retinal Pigment Epithelium
Congenital Grouped Pigmentation ("Bear Tracks")
Metastatic Tumors to the Choroid
Choroidal Melanomas

Choroidal Nevi

Choroidal nevi are usually flat, well-circumscribed lesions that vary in color from brown to grey to black and vary between 0.5 disc diameters to 8 disc diameters in size. Most choroidal nevi are considered flat, but on occasion may be up to 2 mm in thickness. The edges of choroidal nevi can be sharply demarcated or feathery.

Although choroidal nevi are considered to be benign lesions, they may be responsible for a variety of changes in overlying tissues, including degeneration of the retinal pigment epithelium, and photoreceptor cells (including visual field defects), drusen formation, cystoid retinal degeneration, subretinal neovascularization with serous and hemorrhagic detachments of the neurosensory retina. On occasion, subretinal exudates are noted in a circinate pattern. Orange pigment, that is, lipofuscin seen in malignant melanomas can also be noted in some choroidal nevi.

Choroidal nevi tend to grow most rapidly during adolescence and obtain their deepest pigmentation in adulthood. About 30% of adults have choroidal nevi with a 1 in 5000 chance that the nevus will transform into a malignant melanoma. There is no particular sexual predilection for choroidal nevi, but their incidence is higher in Caucasians than in blacks.

Congenital Hypertrophy of the Retinal Pigment Epithelium

Congenital hypertrophy of the retinal pigment epithelium (CHRPE) is a discoid flat-shaped lesion at the level of the retinal pigment epithelium. It may occur as a single lesion or it may occur in a multifocal form termed *congenital grouped pigmentation* or "bear tracks," discussed in the following section. Histologically both conditions appear to be identical.

Solitary CHRPE lesions are usually asymptomatic and dark black and may contain areas of depigmentation (lacunae) within the lesion. The borders of the lesion are sharply defined and often there is a thin halo of depigmentation at the edges of the lesion site. CHRPE lesions are usually 1 to 2 disc diameters in size at the posterior pole and much larger when located in the retinal periphery.

Histologically, there is hyperpigmentation in the region of the CHRPE lesion site and the retinal pigment epithelium cells, although taller, are still only one layer in thickness often containing more pigment granules, which are larger and more globular in shape than the granules within normal retinal pigment epithelium cells nearby. The halo at the edge of the CHRPE lesion is depigmented due to the lack of granules within the retinal pigment epithelium at that site. The overlying neurosensory retina shows degenerative changes, which are probably responsible for the visual field deficits present, otherwise changes in overlying retinal tissues are minimal. Drusen and lipofuscin deposits are rarely seen, and the overlying retinal vessels are usually normal. Visual field deficits can be noted with careful perimetry testing.

Congenital hypertrophy of the retinal pigment epithelium is a unilateral lesion, considered to be benign and stationary with little tendency to grow. If and when these lesions do grow, they do so very slowly. The most important point about CHRPE lesions is that they be recognized for what they really are, and they must be differentiated from choroidal nevi and choroidal melanomas.

Pigmentary Lesions of the Peripheral Retina   Plate 47

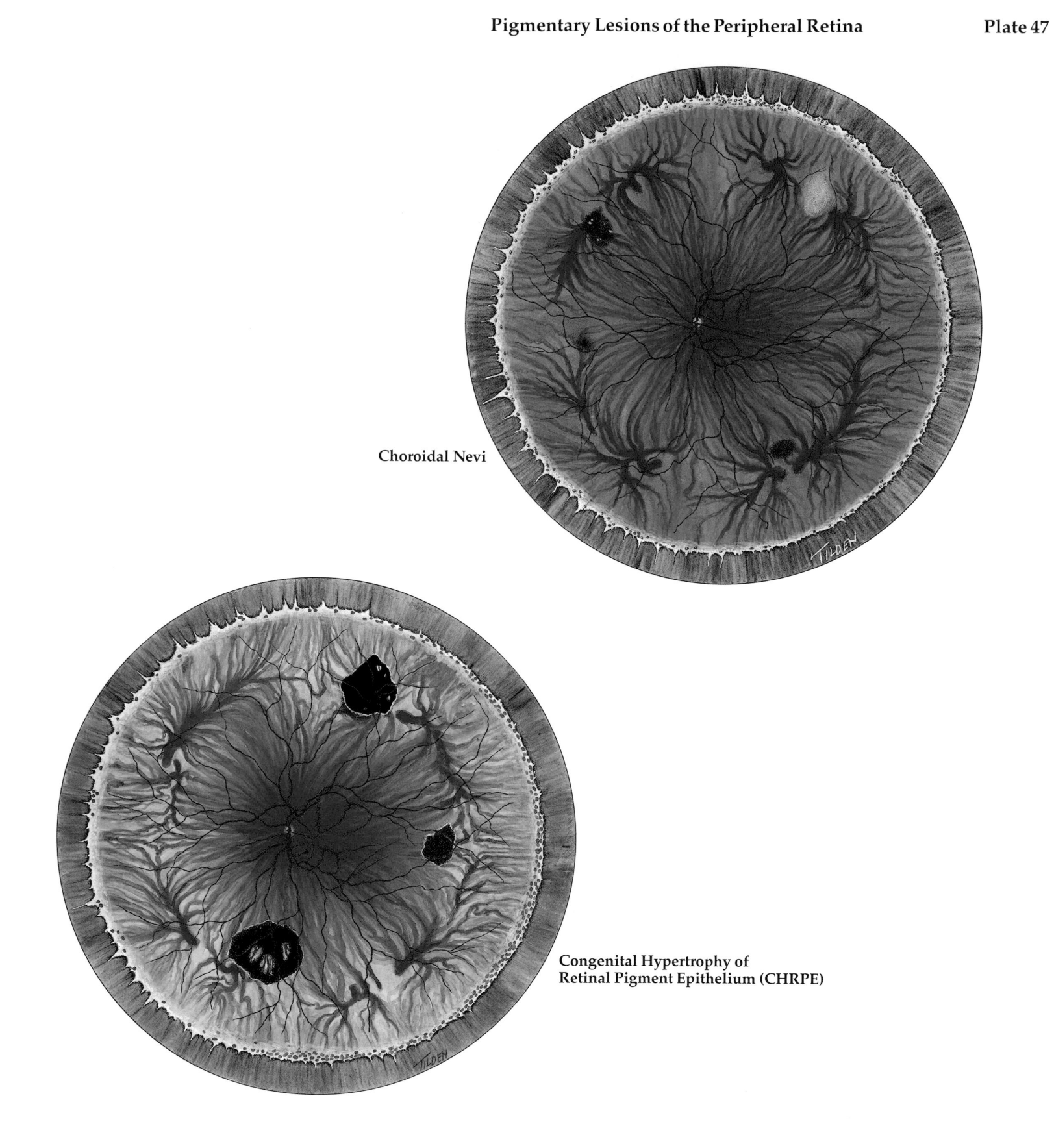

Choroidal Nevi

Congenital Hypertrophy of
Retinal Pigment Epithelium (CHRPE)

Plate 48   **Congenital Grouped Pigmentation ("Bear Tracks")**

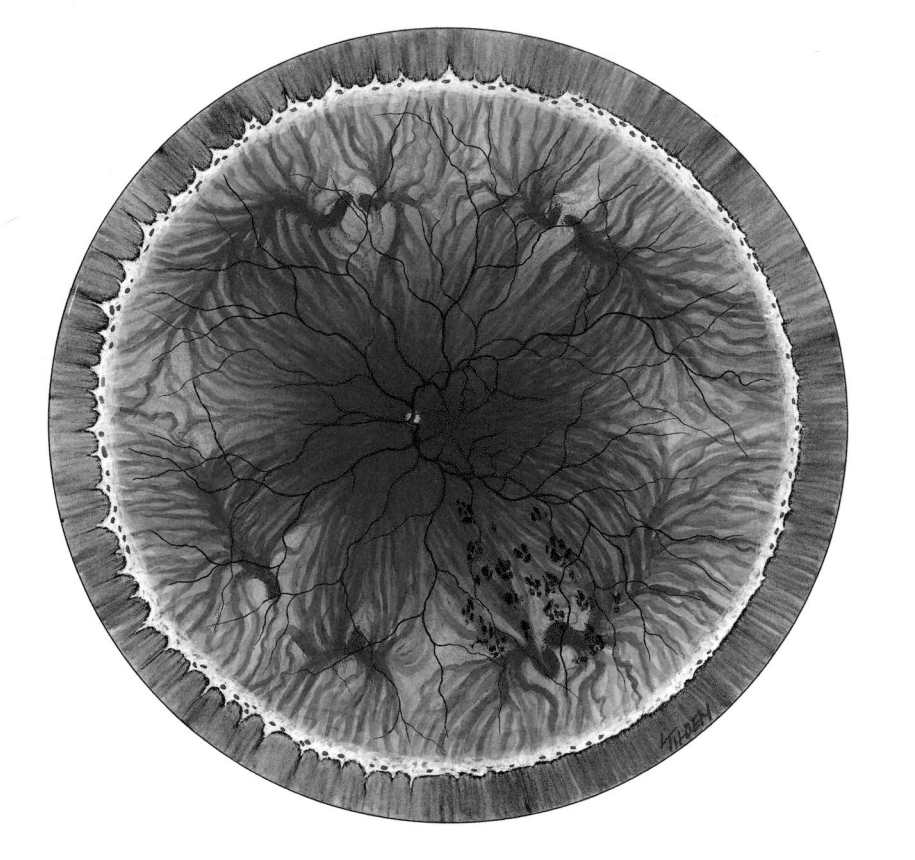

Congenital Grouped Pigmentation ("Bear Tracks")

Congenital grouped pigmentation is a series of pigmented plaquelike lesions that are oval in shape and are due to hyperpigmentation of the retinal pigment epithelium (increased numbers of intracellular pigment granules). The overlying retina is normal. The lesions have sharply defined borders and vary in color from brown to black. The lesions occur in clusters, which appear wider as one goes toward the periphery and are usually located in a sector or quadrant of retina. The clustered arrangement of these multifocal lesions resemble paw prints of an animal and therefore have been termed "bear tracks."

The patient is usually asymptomatic, and the lesions are considered benign and identical to the solitary lesions found in congenital hypertrophy of the retinal pigment epithelium (CHRPE). There is no particular sexual predilection. The differential diagnosis of multifocal CHRPE includes retinal pigment dispersion from inflammation or from trauma as well as sector retinitis pigmentosa.

Metastatic Tumors to the Choroid

Tumors that metastasize to the globe usually do so via the bloodstream and often involve some part of the uveal tract. Metastasis directly to the retina are extremely rare. Metastases to the peripheral choroid are less common than to the posterior pole region. Although some studies indicate a slight predilection of uveal metastasis for the left eye, there is in fact no statistically significant left-right predilection demonstrable.

Metastatic tumors to the uveal tract are rare in children and are therefore found, for the most part, in adults. Breast carcinoma is the most frequent tumor to metastasize to the eye, therefore uveal metastases occur more frequently in women. Lung carcinoma is the second most common primary tumor to metastasize to the eye, followed by gastrointestinal tract and kidney carcinomas. Sarcomas rarely metastasize to the globe. On occasion, a skin melanoma may metastasize to the uveal tract (approximately one in two hundred cases).

Ophthalmoscopically, metastatic choroidal tumors can be flat, irregular in shape or, less commonly, dome-shaped, poorly pigmented, or amelanotic. Typically, the lesions are multifocal, multinodular, and often bilateral, especially if the primary tumor is breast carcinoma. In many metastatic tumors, there is a typical geographic distribution of brown pigmentation on the lesion's inner surface. There is also a serous detachment of the retina, which is often greater in size relative to the tumor size than would be found in a primary choroidal melanoma.

Fluorescein angiography, ultrasonography, ^{32}P testing and a comprehensive medical examination in addition to indirect ophthalmoscopy are important in establishing the diagnosis and plan of treatment for the patient. The differential diagnosis of metastatic tumors of the choroid is similar to that listed for choroidal melanomas in Table 10.1 (page 100).

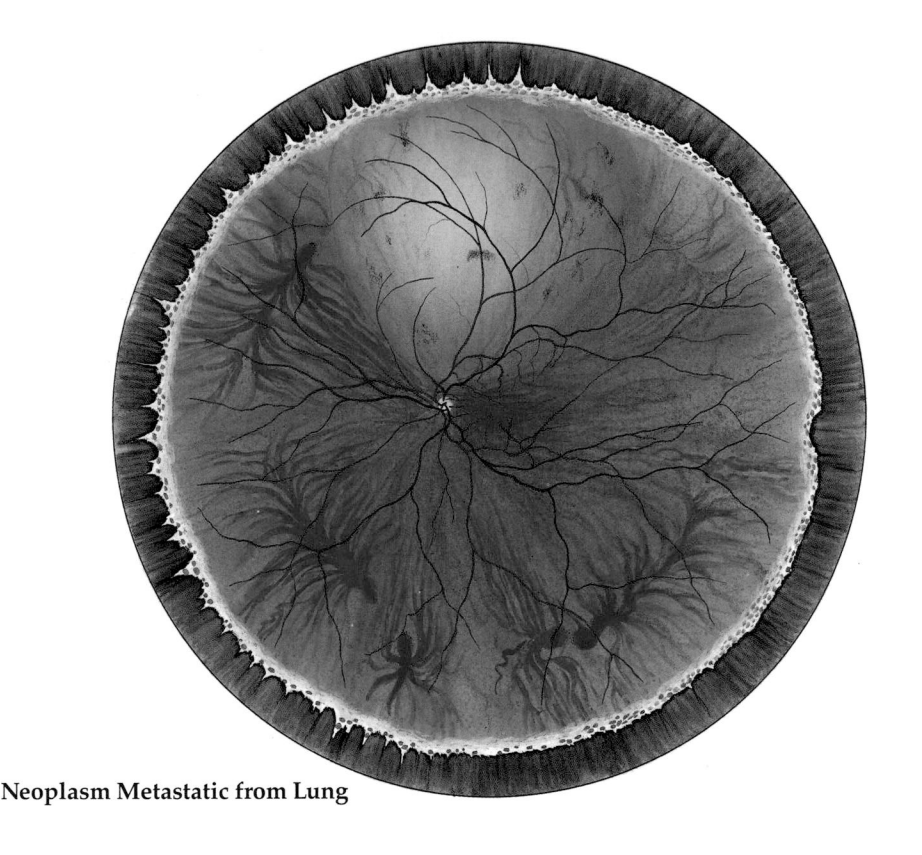

Neoplasm Metastatic from Lung

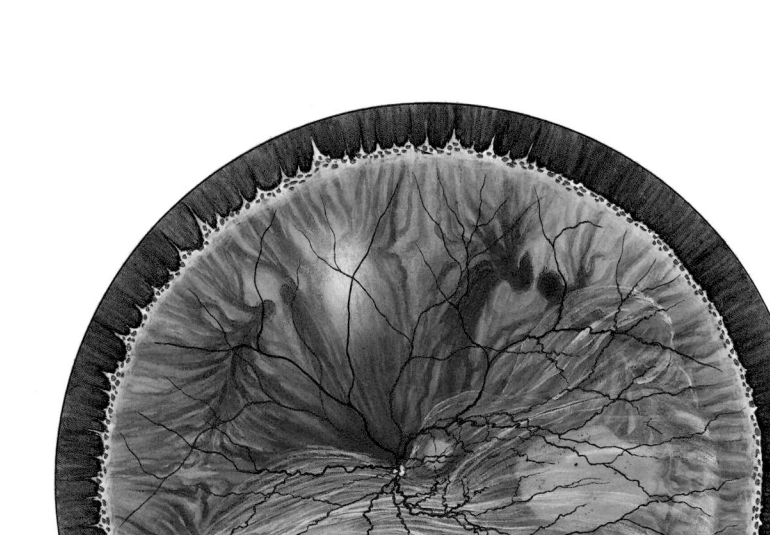

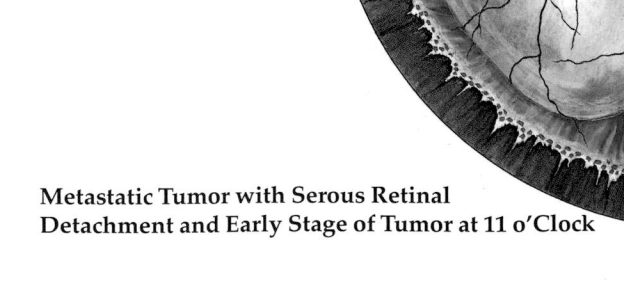

Metastatic Tumor with Serous Retinal Detachment and Early Stage of Tumor at 11 o'Clock

Choroidal Melanomas

Melanomas of the uveal tract are considered to be the most common primary intraocular tumor that affects older adults and is usually diagnosed between the fourth and seventh decades. There is no particular sexual predilection. The melanoma is usually unilateral, and there is no preference for either the left or the right eye. Bilateral cases of melanoma are very rare.

Peripheral choroidal melanomas are asymptomatic when they are small and usually do not interfere with a patient's vision. The lesions are elevated and vary in color from dark brown to grey or even to a creamy yellow (amelanotic). Choroidal melanomas tend to be larger (greater than 5 mm in diameter) than choroidal nevi and are at least 2 mm in height. A localized serous detachment of the retina in and around the melanoma may be present and provide visual symptoms.

Larger choroidal melanomas may break through Bruch's membrane in a mushroom configuration, leading to a serous or exudative retinal detachment. Also, subretinal and intraretinal hemorrhages may occur. In some cases, there is breakthrough bleeding, and a vitreous hemorrhage with sudden visual loss may be the initial findings on examination. That is why ultrasonography should be carried out in adult patients who present with a vitreous hemorrhage in which the media are too cloudy to carry out thorough indirect ophthalmoscopy.

Peripheral choroidal melanomas have poorly defined borders and have several different types of growth patterns. The smaller tumors may be oval, whereas the larger tumors that penetrate Bruch's membrane often have a mushroom shape. The larger tumors often have an associated serous retinal detachment. In some instances, the tumor may actually abut the posterior lens capsule and indent the posterior surface of the lens. The retinal pigment epithelium overlying the choroidal tumor often has pigmentary changes (drusen) and may develop an orange pigment, which has been identified as lipofuscin. Cystoid degeneration of the overlying neurosensory retina is also a common finding.

The Callender classification has defined six categories of melanoma as follows: (1) spindle A, (2) spindle B, (3) fascicular, (4) mixed, (5) necrotic, and (6) epithelioid. Fluorescein angiography, ultrasonography, ^{32}P testing, and a complete medical examination are important modalities in establishing the diagnosis and extent of tumor involvement in a given individual. However, it is not possible, at this time, to tell from these tests and from the ophthalmoscopic appearance of the choroidal melanoma which tissue type one is dealing with, thereby making patient management much more difficult. The differential diagnostic entities to be considered in peripheral uveal melanomas are listed in Table 10.1.

Table 10.1.

Differential Diagnosis of Peripheral Uveal Melanomas

Choroidal nevus

Rhegmatogenous retinal detachment

Choroidal effusion syndrome

Choroidal detachment

Choroidal hemorrhage

Subretinal hemorrhage

Metastatic tumor

Congenital hypertrophy of the retinal pigment epithelium

Choroidal hemangioma

Prehyaloid hemorrhage

Peripheral exudative hemorrhagic chorioretinopathy

Posterior scleritis

Occult intraocular foreign body

Benign reactive lymphoid hyperplasia of the uveal tract

Choroidal Melanomas   **Plate 50**

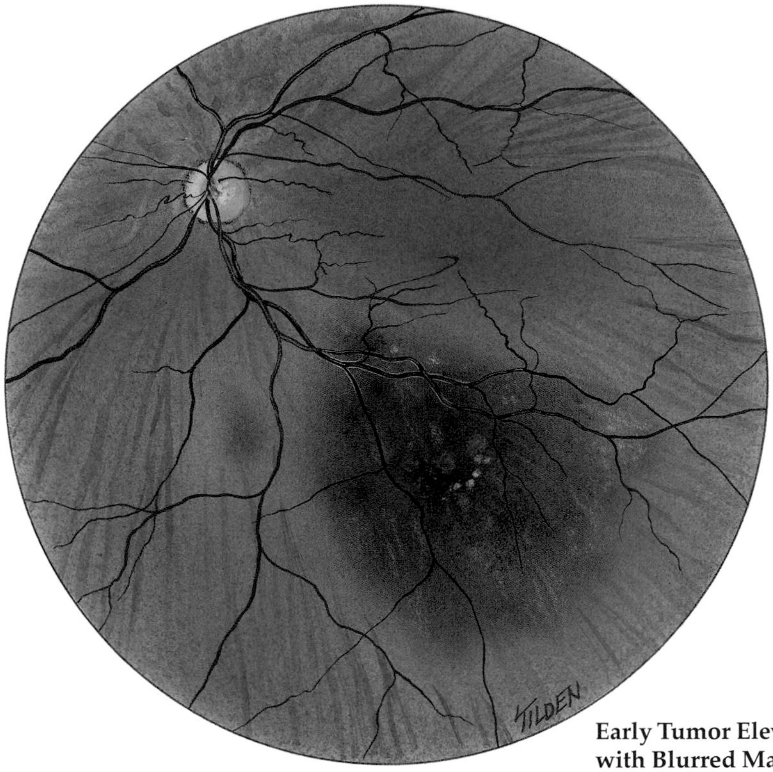

Small Tumor with Localized Retinal Detachment (Posterior Pole)

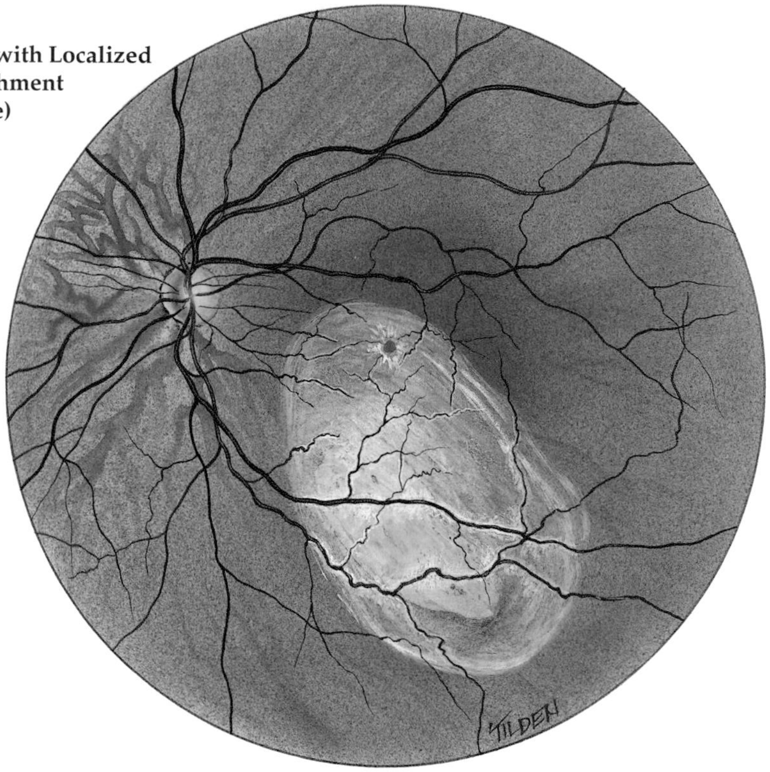

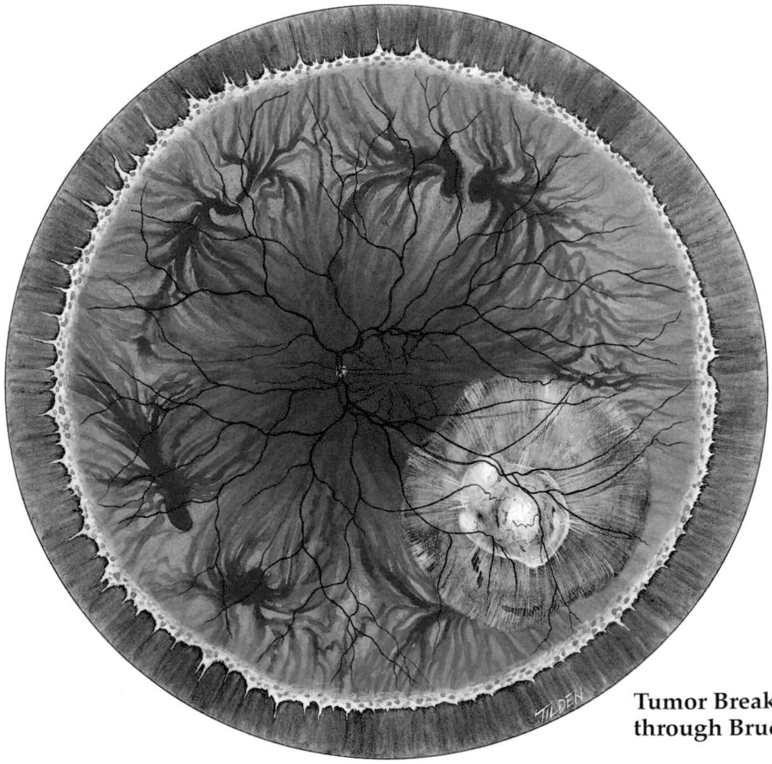

Early Tumor Elevation with Blurred Margins (Posterior Pole)

Large Tumor with Serous Detachment of the Retina

Tumor Breaking through Bruch's Membrane

Retinitis Pigmentosa 11

Retinitis pigmentosa is a progressive primary pigmentary dystrophy of the retina characterized by a collection of bone spicule-shaped pigment located in the midperiphery of the retina, a marked narrowing of the retinal arterioles, night blindness, altered dark adaptation, a diminished electroretinogram, and constricted visual fields (ring scotomas). The retinal veins appear normal in retinitis pigmentosa, as do the optic nerve heads and the maculae initially. However, as the disease progresses, optic pallor (waxy) usually will develop and in some cases cystoid macular edema with macular atrophy also will be present.

There are wide variations in the appearance of the fundus in patients with retinitis pigmentosa. The disease is usually bilateral and involves all four quadrants of the fundus. Cases of unilateral and sector retinitis pigmentosa have been reported. In some cases there is lack of abnormal fundus pigmentation, which has been termed retinitis pigmentosa sine pigments.

Retinitis pigmentosa has autosomal recessive, autosomal dominant, and sex-linked recessive (the most disabling) modes of inheritance and can also be sporadic. The disease usually starts in the first decade of life with the appearance of finely pigmented dots in the midperiphery of the fundus and slowly progresses to the bone-spicule pigment architecture with the development of a ring scotoma. Electroretinogram changes usually precede ophthalmoscopic changes in retinitis pigmentosa.

There is a higher incidence of myopia (75 %), posterior subcapsular lens opacities (up to 60 %), and chronic open-angle glaucoma (3 %) in retinitis pigmentosa patients. In addition to optic atrophy, drusen and hamartomas of the optic nerve head have been noted. Strabismus, progressive external ophthalmoplegia, keratoconus, and microphthalmos have been found in related syndromes.

With increasing age, there is progressive opacification and degeneration of the vitreous. Increased pigment deposits have been observed of the vitreous. Retinal tears and detachments are infrequent in retinitis pigmentosa patients.

There are a number of disorders that comprise the differential diagnosis of retinitis pigmentosa. These are listed in Table 11.1.

Table 11.1.

Differential Diagnosis of Retinitis Pigmentosa

Laurence-Moon syndrome
Bardet-Biedl syndrome
Bassen-Kornzweig syndrome
Refsum's syndrome
Usher's syndrome
Friedreich's ataxia
Goldmann-Favre disease
Hallgren's syndrome
Cockayne's syndrome
Pelizaeus-Merzbacher syndrome
Mucopolysaccharidoses
   Type I   (Hurler's syndrome)
   Type II (Hunter's syndrome)
   Type III (Sanfilippo's syndrome)
   Type IV (Morquio's syndrome)
Congenital rubella
Syphilis
Cystinosis
Myotonic dystrophy
Neuronal ceroid lipofuscinosis
Trauma
Turner's syndrome
Lignac-Fanconi syndrome
Leber's congenital amaurosis
Kearns-Sayre syndrome
Drug toxicities
   Phenothiazines
   Chloroquine
   Vitamin A

Retinitis Pigmentosa   **Plate 51**

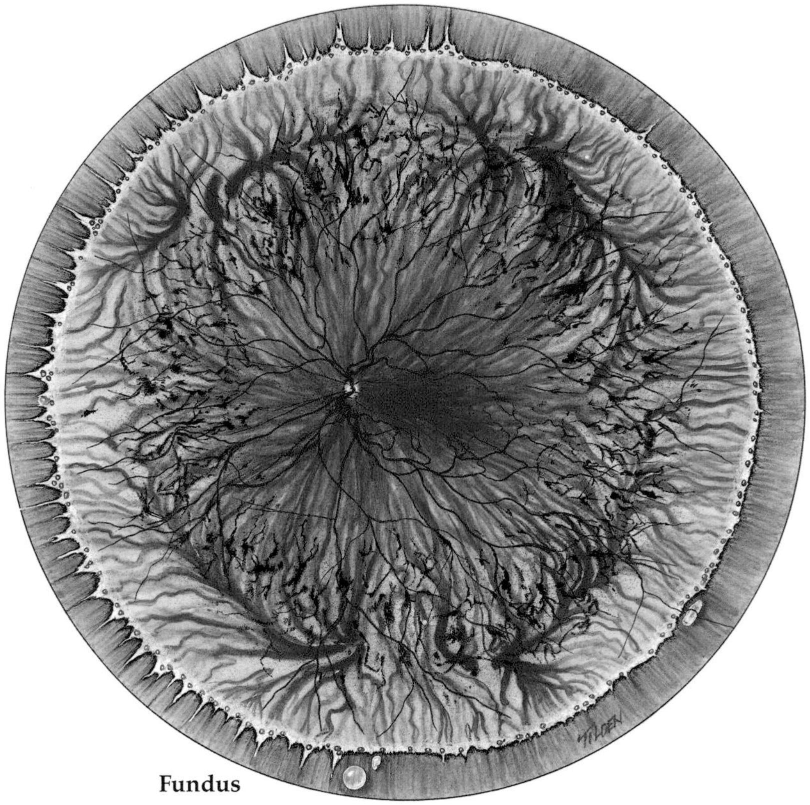

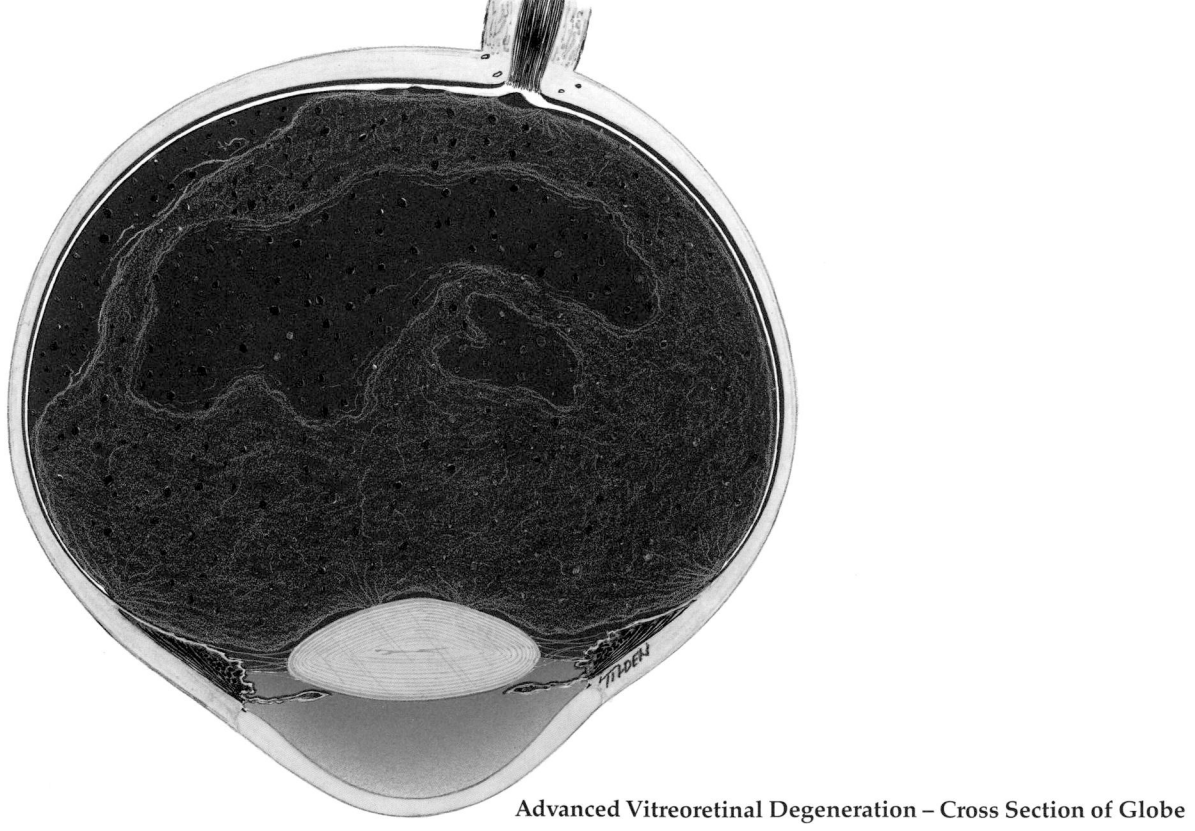

Fundus

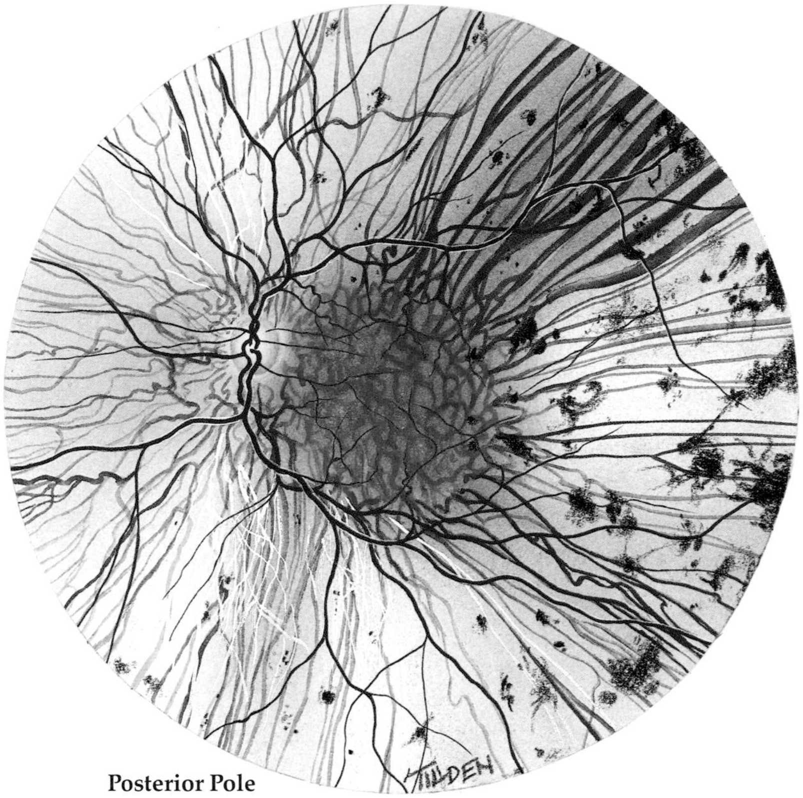

Posterior Pole

Advanced Vitreoretinal Degeneration – Cross Section of Globe

Plate 51   **Retinitis Pigmentosa**

Progressive Vitreoretinal Degeneration – Stage I

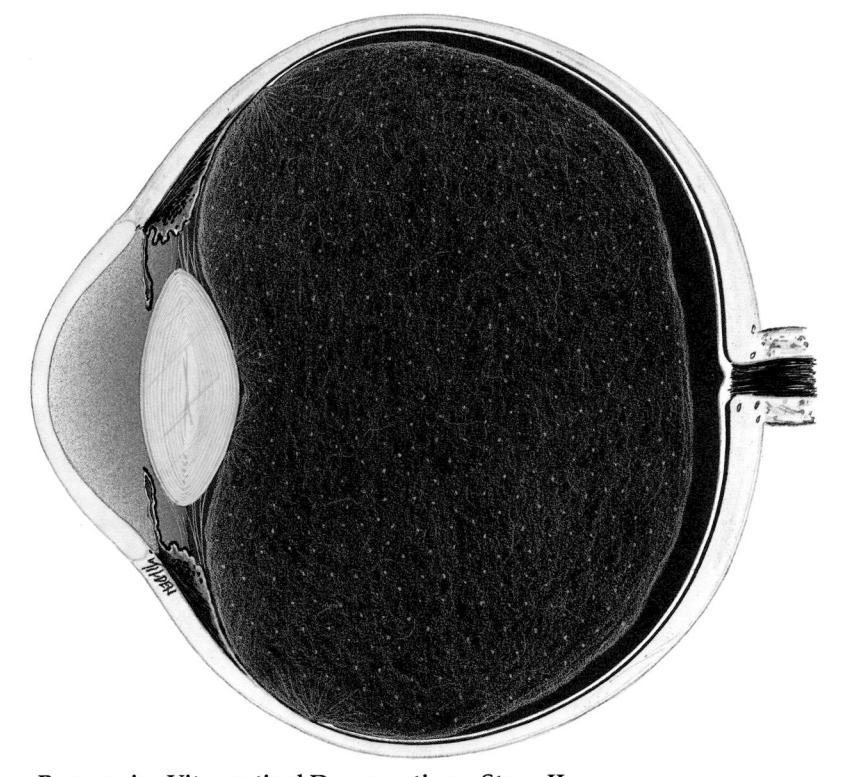

Progressive Vitreoretinal Degeneration – Stage II

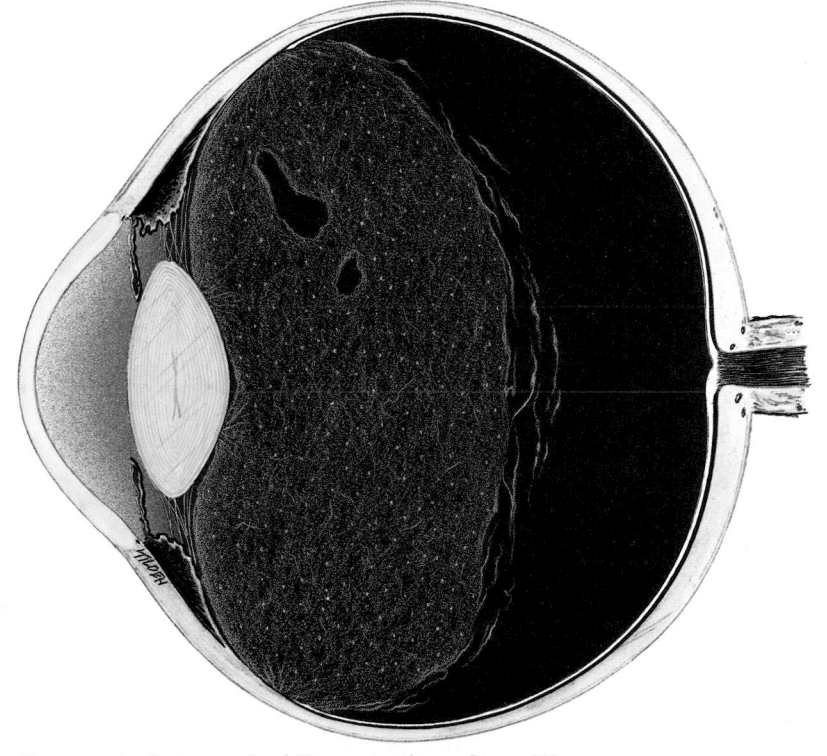

Progressive Vitreoretinal Degeneration – Stage III

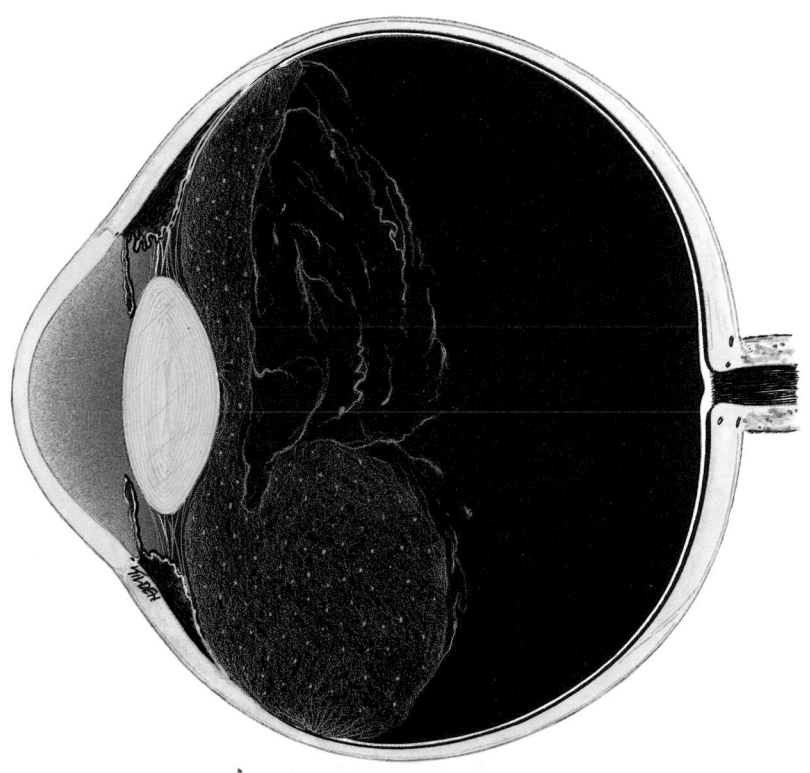

Progressive Vitreoretinal Degeneration – Stage IV

Developmental Disorders: Colobomas of the Retina and Choroid

12

Plate 52   **Coloboma of the Retina and Choroid**

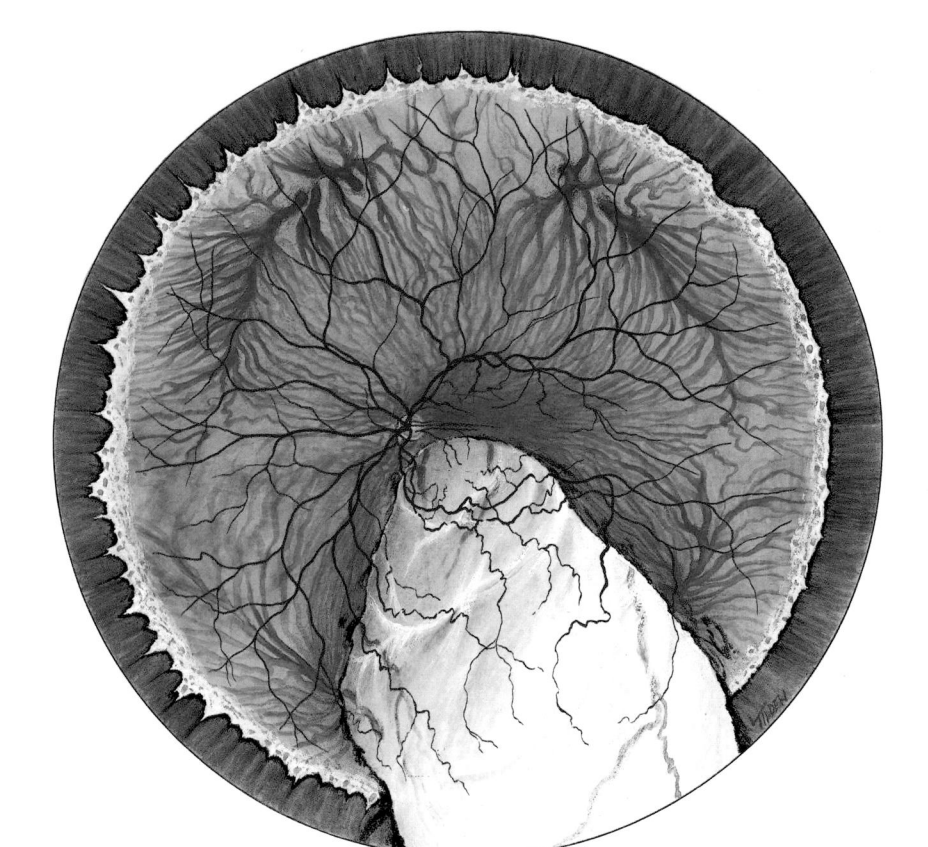

Colobomas of the retina and choroid (0.14% incidence) represent a developmental abnormality usually involving the closure of the fetal fissure during embryonic development. Colobmas can involve the optic nervehead, retina, choroid, ciliary body, lens, and iris tissue. The mechanism of coloboma formation is still not well understood, but has been associated, in some cases, with chromosomal defects such as trisomy 13 and trisomy 18, as well as with use of toxic drugs such as thalidomide.

Ophthalmoscopically, the coloboma region apears to be almost devoid of retinal and choroidal tissues, making the subjacent sclera easily visible. There is a rudimentary membrane containing retinal tissue and vessels that may cover the inner surface of some colobomas. At the edges of a coloboma there is often a highly pigmented border.

Colobomas tend to be bilateral (50% of cases) and typical colobomas are usually in the inferonasal quadrant. Atypical colobomas may be present in the superior quadrants. No specific hereditary patterns have been established for colobomas in general, but there are reports of sporadic cases as well as autosomal dominant and autosomal recessive transmission.

Colobomas may give rise to retinal detachments in 40% of cases. The retinal break may lie within the colobomatous (depigmented) area, making its visualization extremely difficult. Scleral buckling surgery is used to treat retinal detachments in eyes with colobomas of the retina and choroid, but the visual prognosis in these cases is poor compared to the patient with routine rhegmatogenous retinal detachment.

Long-Standing Retinal Detachments

13

Intraocular Fibrosis
Demarcation Lines

Long-standing retinal detachments often have a variety of characteristic structural changes, for example, demarcation lines, macrocysts, and subretinal bands, which are discussed in this chapter.

Intraocular Fibrosis

Intraocular fibrosis may be found in acute as well as chronic cases of retinal detachment and is due to abnormal cellular proliferation in the vitreous gel and the neurosensory retina. Abnormal membranes may also be found on the preretinal and subretinal surfaces of the neurosensory retina. Intraocular fibrosis may also take place within the neurosensory retina in such conditions as star folds and macular pucker.

The cellular origins of abnormal vitreoretinal membranes are listed in Table 13.1. In most cases, the membranes are derived from either the Müller (glial) cells or the retinal pigment epithelium.

Abnormal cellular proliferation leads to membrane formation, which may, in turn, undergo a contraction process, leading to folds in the retina, localized traction, and/or rhegmatogenous retinal detachments. Extramacular retinal folds are termed *star folds*; abnormal folds within the macula are termed *macular pucker*.

In some cases, there is a relentless progression of these membranes, leading to *proliferative vitreoretinopathy (PVR)* or *massive periretinal proliferation (MPP)*, wherein the entire retina is thrown into a large funnel-shaped star fold whose apex is at the optic nerve head. In these cases, there is extensive liquefaction or syneresis of the vitreous gel posteriorly with an increased condensation of the anterior vitreous gel (at the base of the funnel). A simple classification of proliferative vitreoretinopathy is outlined in Table 13.2.

Table 13.1.
Cellular Sources of Vitreoretinal Membranes

Whole blood
  Lymphocytes
  Leukocytes
  Monocytes
  Platelets

Vascular endothelium

Ciliary body (nonpigmented epithelium)

Fibroblasts

Hyalocytes

Retinal pigment epithelium (fibroblastic transformation)

Müller cells (glial)

Table 13.2.
The Classification of Retinal Detachment with Proliferative Vitreoretinopathy (PVR)

Grade	Name	Clinical Signs
A	Minimal	Vitreous haze, vitreous pigment clumps
B	Moderate	Wrinkling of the inner retinal surface, rolled edge of retinal break, retinal stiffness, vessel tortuosity
C	Marked	Full thickness fixed retinal folds
C-1		One quadrant
C-2		Two quadrants
C-3		Three quadrants
D	Massive	Fixed retinal folds in four quadrants
D-1		Wide funnel shape
D-2		Narrow funnel shape*
D-3		Closed funnel (optic nervehead not visible)

* Narrow funnel shape exists when the anterior end of the funnel can be seen by indirect ophthalmoscopy within the 45° field of a +20D condensing lens (Nikon or equivalent).
Reprinted with permission from The Retina Society Terminology Committee: The classification of retinal detachment with proliferative vitreoretinopathy. Ophthalmology 90 (2): 121–5. Philadelphia, Lippincott/Harper & Row, 1983

Proliferative Vitreoretinopathy (PVR) **Plate 53**

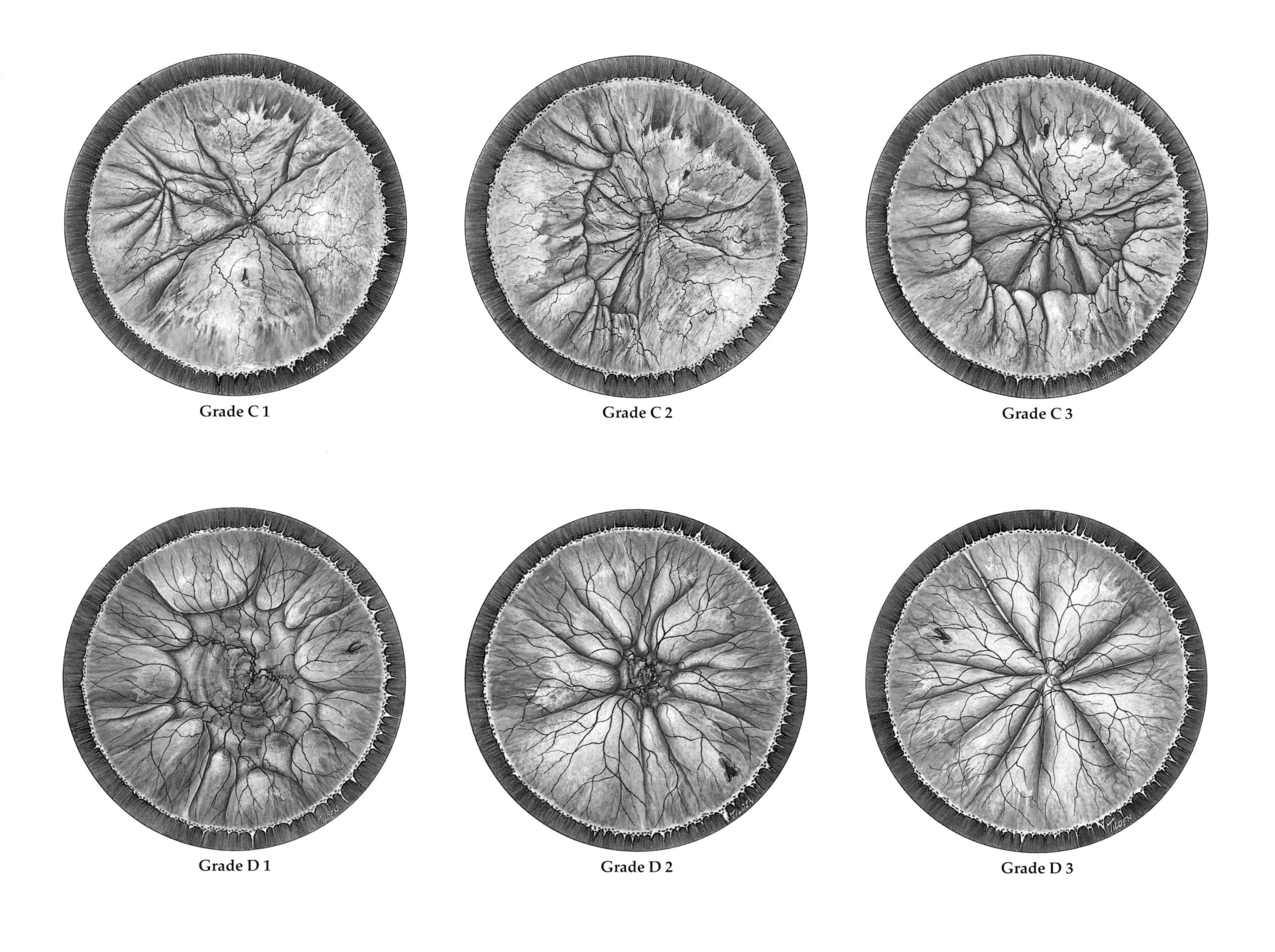

Grade C 1   Grade C 2   Grade C 3

Grade D 1   Grade D 2   Grade D 3

Intraocular fibrosis can lead to a variety of intraocular membranes in the posterior segment of the globe, and their classification is outlined in Table 13.3.

In chronic retinal detachments, there are proliferative and degenerative retinal pigment epithelium changes, including increased pigmentary material in the subretinal fluid, and, in some cases, nonpigmented subretinal strands of tissue are present that act as a hammock supporting overlying detached neurosensory retinal tissue. The ends of these subretinal strands are attached to either the retinal pigment epithelium or to the subretinal surface of the neurosensory retina.

Chronically detached retina tends to be thinner and more transparent than freshly detached retina. The subretinal fluid may be more viscous, and, in cases of tiny retinal breaks, one may see shifting subretinal fluid, which is not seen in fresh rhegmatogenous retinal detachments. Fixed retinal folds and a more rigid detached retina are commonly noted in long-standing retinal detachments. Microcystoid spaces, usually at the level of the outer plexiform and inner nuclear layers, are found in chronically detached retinas. These cystic changes are reversible if the retina is reattached within a reasonable period of time.

In chronic retinal detachments, retinal tear flaps and opercula have an opportunity to degenerate and shrink so that their size is much smaller than the aperture size of the tear site. In contrast, opercula and retinal tear flaps in fresh retinal tears usually are the same size as the retinal tear aperture.

Large *intraretinal macrocysts* can develop in a period of several months to years in a long-standing retinal detachment. These macrocysts are commonly found in inferior retinal detachments due to such conditions as an inferior temporal dialysis of the young. Intraretinal macrocysts are often elevated and protrude into the subretinal space and are found mostly near the equator and only rarely at the posterior pole. The cysts collapse and regress rapidly after surgical reattachment of the retina and do not require direct drainage of the cystic cavity itself.

Table 13.3.

Classification of Intraocular Membranes in the Posterior Segment of the Eye

Lens capsule (remnants) membranes

Cyclitic membranes

Vitreoretinal membranes
  Anteroposterior traction
    Truncated cone membranes
    Stalk membranes
      Optic nerve head
      Retina
  Equatorial traction
    Equatorial membranes
    Bridging membranes
  Epiretinal traction
    Macular pucker
    Extramacular pucker
    Star fold

Intraretinal membranes
  Tangential traction
    Macular pucker
    Extramacular pucker
    Star fold

Subretinal membranes
  Tangential traction
    Clothesline
    Placoid
      Fishnet
      Discoid
    Napkin ring (peripapillary)
  Anteroposterior traction
    Clothesline
    Placoid
      Fishnet
    Napkin ring

Demarcation Lines

Demarcation lines are found in slowly progressive or chronic retinal detachments. In these cases, the amount of subretinal fluid may stabilize for some time. The presence of the subretinal fluid induces an irritation or friction as it moves back and forth, leading to secondary proliferative changes of the retinal pigment epithelium at the boundary line between the attached and detached retina. Fibrous metaplasia of the retinal pigment epithelium may also occur.

Ultimately a hyperpigmented line or, in some cases, a hypopigmented line develops that is termed the demarcation (friction) line. The demarcation line often, but not always, serves as a barrier to the further progression of the retinal detachment. In some eyes, several concentric demarcation lines are present, similiar to high-water marks, indicating several waves of activity or progression of the retinal detachment interspersed with periods of nonprogression or stability. Often demarcation lines form a partial circle and within that circle one usually finds the causative retinal break.

The characteristics of long-standing retinal detachments are outlined in Table 13.4.

Table 13.4.
Characteristics of Long-Standing Retinal Detachments

Detached retina
  Shrinkage of retinal tear flaps and opercula
  Thinning and atrophy (↑ transparency of retina)
  Microcystoid degeneration
  Intraretinal macrocysts
  Fixed folds (PVR)
    ↓ Mobility of retina (↑ rigidity)
  Subretinal fluid
    ↑ Viscosity (↑ protein)
  Pigment debris
  Shifting subretinal fluid (with very small retinal holes)

Retinal pigment epithelium
  Hyperpigmentation
  Hypopigmentation and atrophy
  Fibrous metaplasia
  Fibroplastic transformation (MPP)
  Demarcation line formation

Intraocular fibrosis
  Vitreal membranes
  Preretinal membranes
  Intraneurosensory membranes
    Star folds
    Macular pucker
  Subretinal strands (nonpigmented)
  Proliferative vitreoretinopathy (PVR)

Long-Standing Retinal Detachment with Demarcation Line, Intraretinal Macrocysts and Fixed Retinal Folds

Plate 54

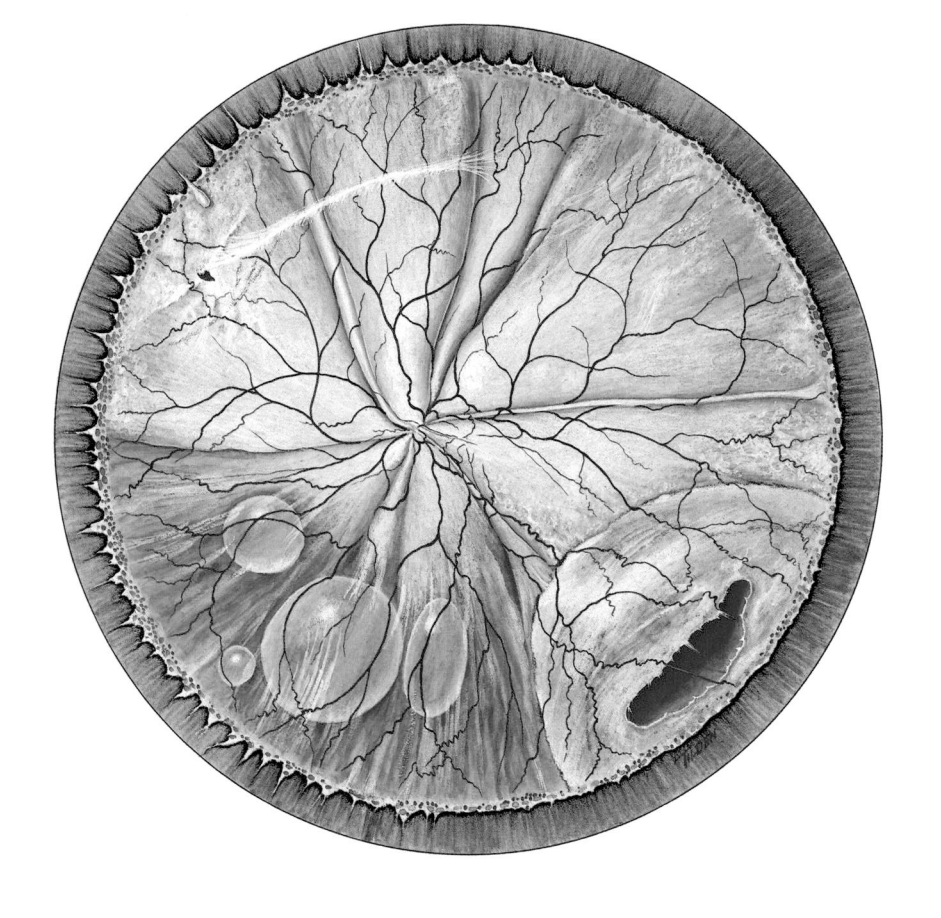

Fundus Color Code   14

Many years ago, Dr. Charles Schepens devised a system of sketching the fundus as a way of recording the findings on indirect ophthalmoscopy with scleral depression. This technique has served as an invaluable aid in improving our comprehension and overall understanding of retinal diseases as well as planning vitreoretinal surgery in specific patients.

As a by-product of the fundus sketching system a universal color code was developed to help standardize and interpret fundus drawings. The fundus code is outlined in Table 14.1. In its simplest form, the fundus color code is organized along the following lines:

Red: attached retina, retinal arterioles, fresh hemorrhage, vortex veins, retinal tears and holes;

Blue: retinal veins, detached retina, outline of the ora serrata, cystoid degeneration;

Green: any opacities in the eye, vitreous hemorrhage, cotton wool patches, vitreous membranes, and intraocular foreign bodies;

Brown: uveal tissue, pars plana cysts, pigment beneath detached retina, choroidal tumors, and choroidal detachments;

Yellow: retinal exudates, intraretinal edema, drusen, post-photocoagulation burns (edema) of the retina;

Black: pigment in choroid, outline of the long and short posterior ciliary vessels and nerves, pigmented demarcation lines at edge of long-standing retinal detachment, pigmented laser photocoagulation scars.

A more comprehensive and detailed description of the fundus color code is provided in Table 14.1. In the pages following the table, the entire fundus color code is illustrated. For each feature listed in Table 14.1 the ophthalmologist's sketch representation is shown side-by-side with a fundus painting of the condition as viewed through the ophthalmoscope.

Table 14.1 Fundus Color Code[1]

Code[2]	Fundus Color and Characteristics	Code[2]	Fundus Color and Characteristics	Code[2]	Fundus Color and Characteristics
[R]	Red *Solid*	[B]	Blue *Solid*	[Br]	Brown *Solid*
1	Retinal arterioles	15	Detached retina	46	Uveal tissue
2	Neovascularization	16	Retinal veins	47	Pars plana cysts
3	Vascular abnormalities or anomalies	17	Outlines of retinal breaks (tears, holes)	48	Ciliary processes (pars plicata)
4	Vortex veins	18	Outline of ora serrata (dentate processes, ora bays)	49	Striae ciliaris
5	Attached retina			50	Pigment beneath detached retina
6	Hemorrhages (preretinal, intraretinal)	19, 20, 21, 22	Meridional [19], radial [20], fixed [21], and circumferential [22] folds	51	Outline of chorioretinal atrophy beneath detached retina
7	Open interior of conventional retinal breaks (tears, holes)	23	Vitreoretinal traction tufts	52	Subretinal, fibrous demarcation lines
8	Open interior of outer layer holes in retinoschisis	24	Retinal granular tags and tufts (cystic, noncystic)	53	Outline of posterior staphyloma
9	Normal macula — drawn as a red dot	25	Outline of flat neovascularization	54	Malignant choroidal melanomas
		26	Outline of lattice degeneration	55	Edge of buckle beneath detached retina
	Crosslined	27	Outline of thin areas of retina	56	Choroidal detachment
10, 11	Open portion of giant tears [10] or large dialyses [11]	28	Intraretinal cysts (with overlying curvilinear stripes to show configuration)		
12	Inner portion of chorioretinal atrophy				
13	Open portion of retinal holes in inner layer of retinoschisis		*Crosslined*	[Y]	Yellow *Solid*
14	Inner portion of thin areas of retina	29	Inner layer of retinoschisis	57	Intraretinal edema
		30	White-with- or -without-pressure (label)	58	Intra- or subretinal hard yellow exudate
		31	Detached pars plana epithelium anterior to separation of ora serrata	59	Deposits in retinal pigmented epithelium
		32	Rolled edges of retinal tears (curved lines)	60	Detached maculae in some retinal separations
				61	Postphotocoagulation retinal edema
			Stippled or circled	62	Substance of long and short posterior ciliary nerves
		33	Cystoid degeneration		
					Stippled or dotted
			Interrupted lines	63	Drusen
		34	Outline of change in area or folds of detached retina because of shifting fluid		
				[Bl]	Black *Solid*
				64, 65, 66	Pigment within detached retina (lattice [64], flap of horseshoe tear [65], paravascular pigment [66])
		[G]	Green *Solid*	67, 68	Pigment in choroid [67] or pigmented epithelial hyperpigmentation in areas of detached retina [68]
		35	Opacities in the media (cornea, anterior chamber, lens, vitreous); label specifically		
		36	Vitreous hemorrhage	69	Pigmented demarcation lines at attached margin of detached retina or within detached retina
		37	Vitreous membranes		
		38	Hyaloid ring	70	Nevi
		39	Intraocular foreign bodies	71, 72	Sheathed vessels outlined or solid black, depending upon extent (lattice [71], retinoschisis [72])
		40	Retinal operculum		
		41	Cotton-wool patches	73	Edge of buckle beneath attached retina
		42	Pearls at the ora serrata	74	Outline of long posterior ciliary vessels and nerves (pigmented)
		43	Outline of elevated neovascularization		
				75	Outline of short ciliary vessels and nerves
			Stippled or dotted	76	Outline of chorioretinal atrophy
		44	Asteroid hyalosis	77	Hyperpigmentation as a result of previous treatment with cryotherapy, photocoagulation, or diathermy
		45	Frosting or snowflakes on cystoid, retinoschisis, or lattice degeneration		

[1] From Morse P: Vitreoretinal Disease. A Manual for Diagnosis and Treatment. Chicago, Year Book Medical Publishers Inc., 1979. Tables 2-1 through 2-6. pp. 41–44.

[2] The numbers given in these columns refer to the specific figures illustrating that feature in the illustrated fundus color code that follows this table.

Fundus Color Code

Color	Feature	Ophthalmologist's Sketch Representation	Ophthalmoscopic Finding	Color Code Number (See Table 14.1)
Red *Solid*	Retinal arterioles			1
	Neovascularization			2
	Vascular abnormalities or anomalies			3
	Vortex veins			4
	Attached retina			5
	Hemorrhages (preretinal, intraretinal)			6

Fundus Color Code

Color	Feature	Ophthalmologist's Sketch Representation	Ophthalmoscopic Finding	Color Code Number (See Table 14.1)
Red *Solid*	Open interior of conventional retinal breaks (tears, holes)	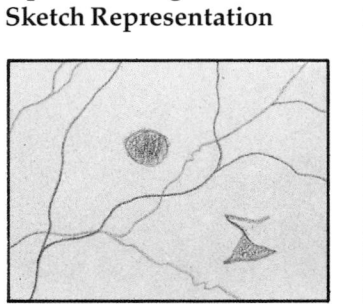		7
	Open interior of outer layer holes in retinoschisis	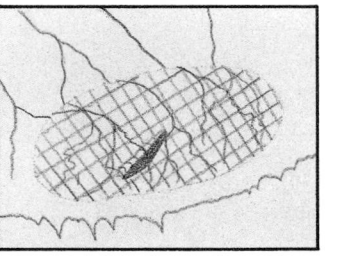		8
	Normal macula-drawn as a red dot	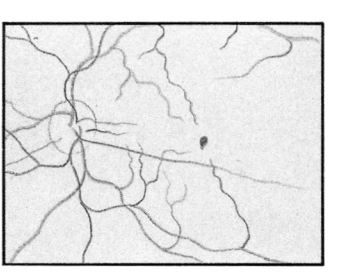		9
Red *Crosslined*	Open portion of giant tears	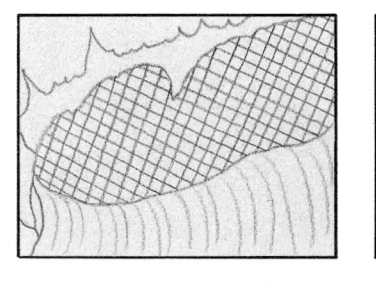	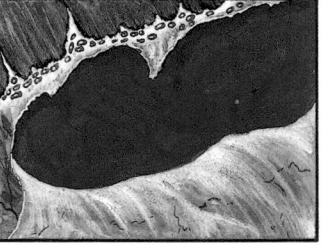	10
	Open portion of large dialyses	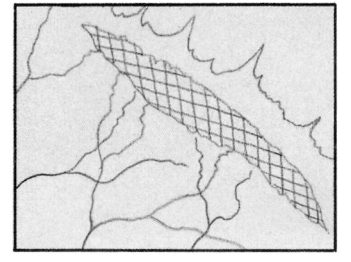	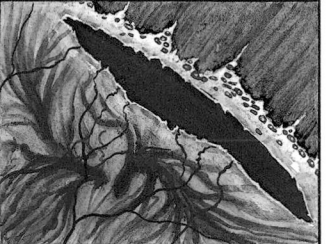	11
	Inner portion of chorioretinal atrophy	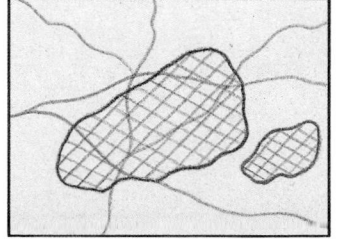	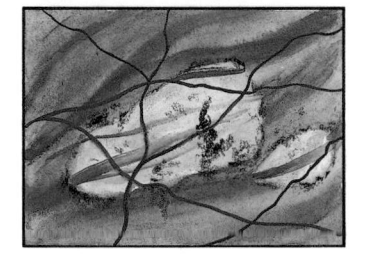	12

Fundus Color Code

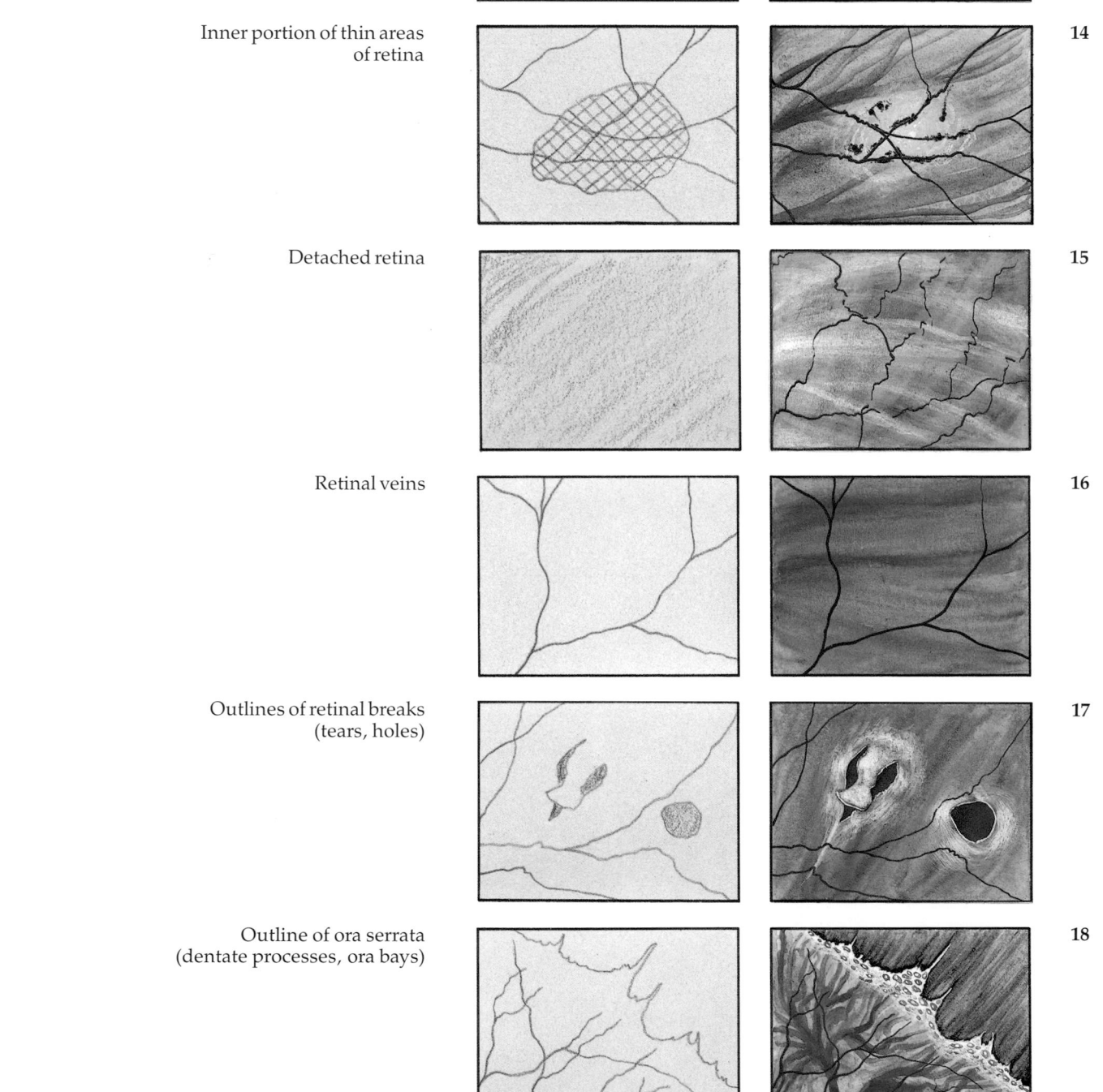

Color	Feature	Ophthalmologist's Sketch Representation	Ophthalmoscopic Finding	Color Code Number (See Table 14.1)
Red *Crosslined*	Open portion of retinal holes in inner layer of retinoschisis			13
	Inner portion of thin areas of retina			14
Blue *Solid*	Detached retina			15
	Retinal veins			16
	Outlines of retinal breaks (tears, holes)			17
	Outline of ora serrata (dentate processes, ora bays)			18

Fundus Color Code

Color	Feature	Ophthalmologist's Sketch Representation	Ophthalmoscopic Finding	Color Code Number (See Table 14.1)
Blue *Solid*	Meridional folds	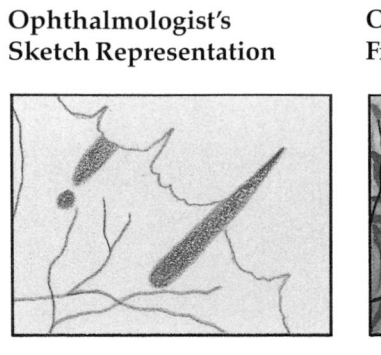		**19**
	Radial folds	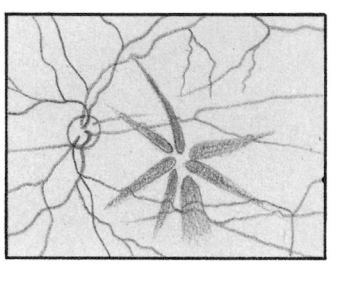	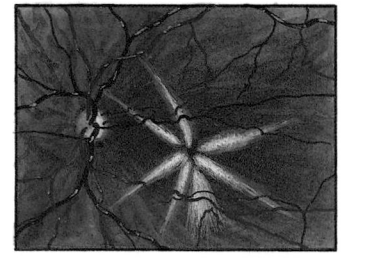	**20**
	Fixed folds	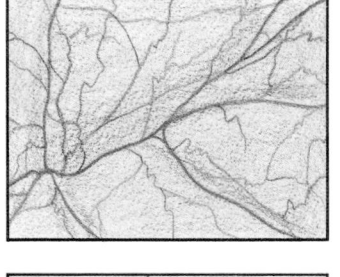	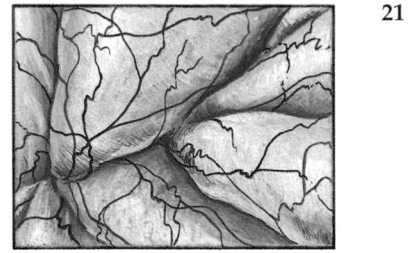	**21**
	Circumferential folds	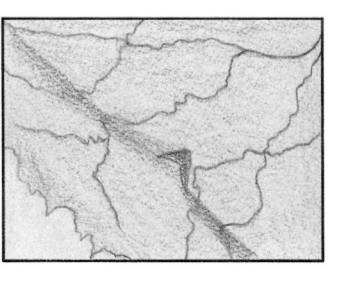		**22**
	Vitreoretinal traction tufts		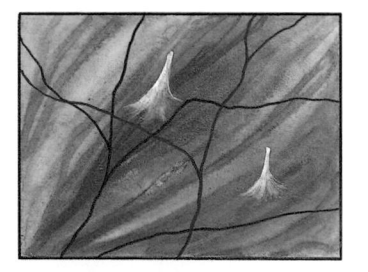	**23**
	Retinal granular tags and tufts (cystic, noncystic)	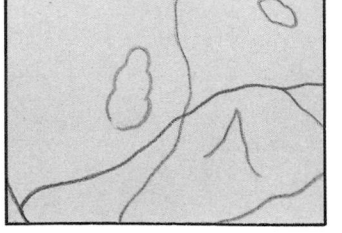		**24**

Fundus Color Code

Color	Feature	Ophthalmologist's Sketch Representation	Ophthalmoscopic Finding	Color Code Number (See Table 14.1)
Blue *Solid*	Outline of flat neovascularization			25
	Outline of lattice degeneration			26
	Outline of thin areas of retina			27
	Intraretinal cysts (with overlying curvilinear stripes to show configuration)			28
Blue *Crosslined*	Inner layer of retinoschisis			29
	White-with- or -without-pressure (label)			30

Fundus Color Code

Color	Feature	Ophthalmologist's Sketch Representation	Ophthalmoscopic Finding	Color Code Number (See Table 14.1)
Blue *Crosslined*	Detached pars plana epithelium anterior to separation of ora serrata			31
	Rolled edges of retinal tears (curved lines)			32
Blue *Stippled or circled*	Cystoid degeneration			33
Blue *Interrupted lines*	Outline of change in area or folds of detached retina because of shifting fluid			34
Green *Solid*	Opacities in the media (cornea, anterior chamber, lens, vitreous); label specifically			35
	Vitreous hemorrhage			36

Fundus Color Code

Color	Feature	Ophthalmologist's Sketch Representation	Ophthalmoscopic Finding	Color Code Number (See Table 14.1)
Green *Solid*	Vitreous membranes	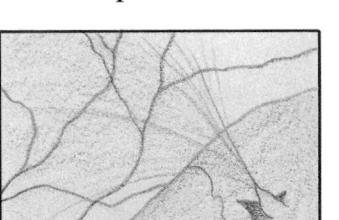	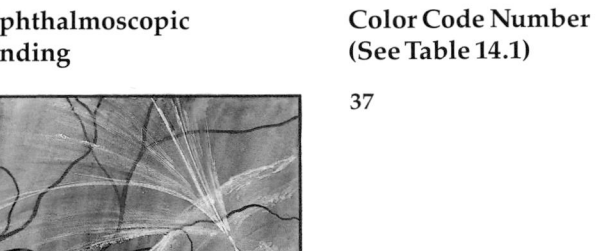	37
	Hyaloid ring			38
	Intraocular foreign bodies		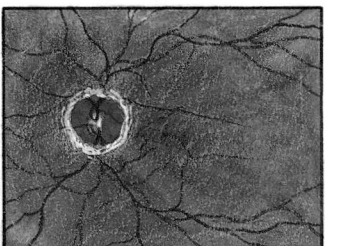	39
	Retinal operculum	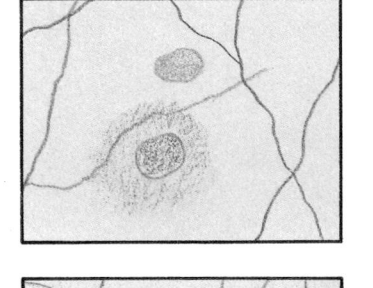	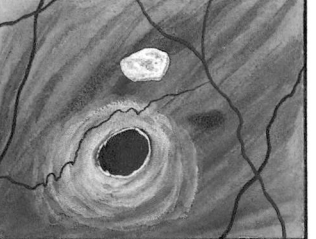	40
	Cotton-wool patches		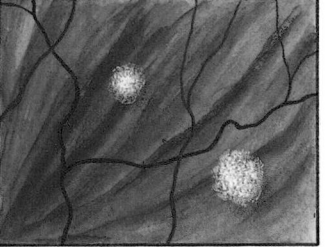	41
	Pearls at the ora serrata	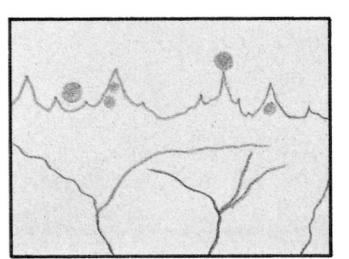		42

Fundus Color Code

Color	Feature	Ophthalmologist's Sketch Representation	Ophthalmoscopic Finding	Color Code Number (See Table 14.1)
Green *Solid*	Outline of elevated neovascularization			43
Green *Stippled or dotted*	Asteroid hyalosis			44
	Frosting or snowflakes on cystoid, retinoschisis, or lattice degeneration			45
Brown *Solid*	Uveal tissue			46
	Pars plana cysts		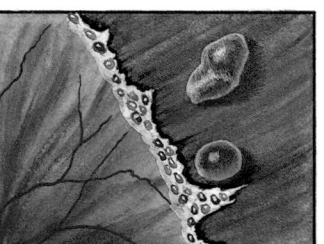	47
	Ciliary processes (pars plicata)	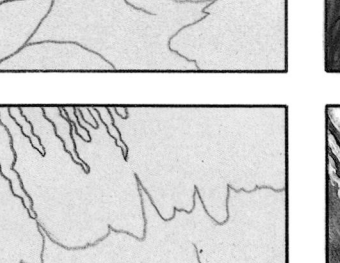		48

Fundus Color Code

Color	Feature	Ophthalmologist's Sketch Representation	Ophthalmoscopic Finding	Color Code Number (See Table 14.1)
Brown *Solid*	Striae ciliaris			49
	Pigment beneath detached retina			50
	Outline of chorioretinal atrophy beneath detached retina			51
	Subretinal, fibrous demarcation lines			52
	Outline of posterior staphyloma			53
	Malignant choroidal melanomas			54

Fundus Color Code

Color	Feature	Ophthalmologist's Sketch Representation	Ophthalmoscopic Finding	Color Code Number (See Table 14.1)
Brown *Solid*	Edge of buckle beneath detached retina			55
	Choroidal detachment			56
Yellow *Solid*	Intraretinal edema			57
	Intra- or subretinal hard yellow exudate			58
	Deposits in retinal pigmented epithelium			59
	Detached maculae in some retinal separations			60

Fundus Color Code

Color	Feature	Ophthalmologist's Sketch Representation	Ophthalmoscopic Finding	Color Code Number (See Table 14.1)
Yellow *Solid*	Postphotocoagulation retinal edema			**61**
	Substance of long and short posterior ciliary nerves			**62**
Yellow *Stippled or dotted*	Drusen			**63**
Black *Solid*	Pigment within detached retina (lattice)			**64**
	Pigment within detached retina (flap of horseshoe tear)			**65**
	Pigment within detached retina (paravascular pigment)			**66**

Fundus Color Code

Color	Feature	Ophthalmologist's Sketch Representation	Ophthalmoscopic Finding	Color Code Number (See Table 14.1)
Black *Solid*	Pigment in choroid	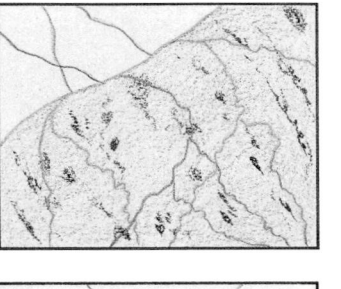	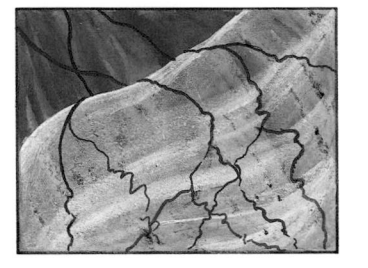	**67**
	Pigmented epithelial hyperpigmentation in areas of detached retina		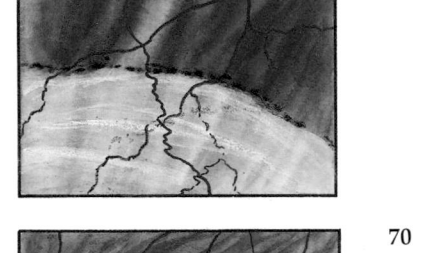	**68**
	Pigmented demarcation lines at attached margin of detached retina or within detached retina			**69**
	Nevi	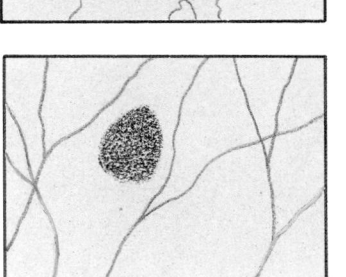		**70**
	Sheathed vessels outlined or solid black, depending upon extent (lattice)	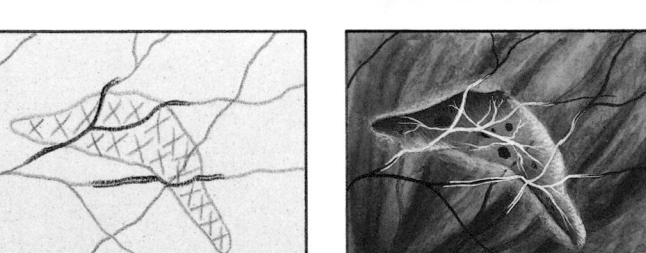	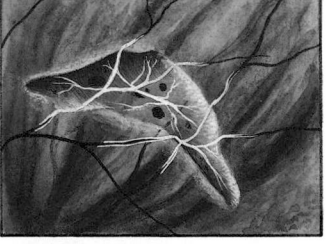	**71**
	Sheathed vessels outlined or solid black, depending upon extent (retinoschisis)	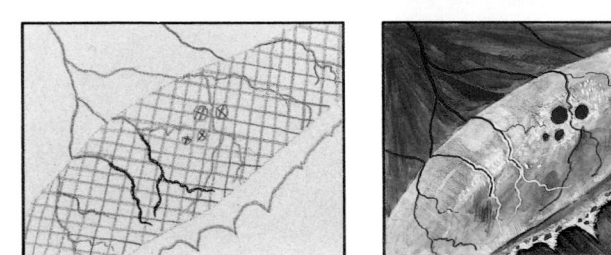		**72**

Fundus Color Code

Color	Feature	Ophthalmologist's Sketch Representation	Ophthalmoscopic Finding	Color Code Number (See Table 14.1)
Black *Solid*	Edge of buckle beneath attached retina	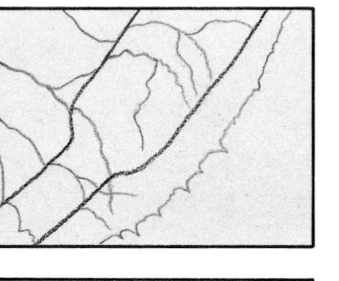	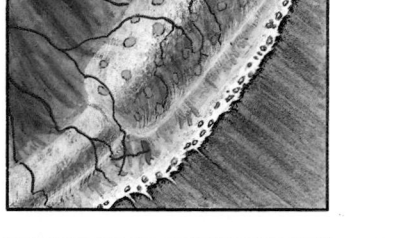	73
	Outline of long posterior ciliary vessels and nerves (pigmented)			74
	Outline of short ciliary vessels and nerves			75
	Outline of chorioretinal atrophy	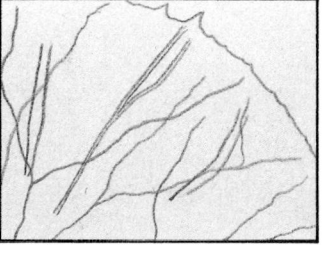	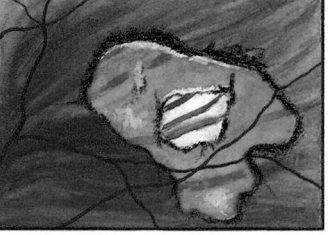	76
	Hyperpigmentation as a result of previous treatment with cryotherapy, photocoagulation or diathermy	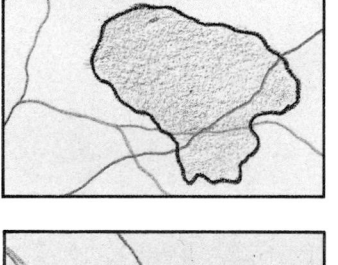		77

Bibliographies and References

General Bibliography

Apple DJ, Raab MF: Clinicopathologic Correlation of Ocular Disease. A Text and Stereoscopic Atlas, 2nd ed. St. Louis, Mosby, 1978. 526 pp

Bell FC, Stenstrom WS: Atlas of the Peripheral Retina. Philadelphia, Saunders, 1983. 232 pp

Benson WE: Retinal Detachment. Diagnosis and Management. Hagerstown, MD, Harper & Row, 1980. 196 pp

Byer NE: The Peripheral Retina in Profile. A Stereoscopic Atlas. Torrence, CA, Criterion Press, 1982. 159 pp

Chignell AH: Retinal Detachment Surgery. New York, Springer-Verlag, 1980. 166 pp

Curtin BJ: The Myopias: Basic Science and Clinical Management. Philadelphia, Harper & Row, 1985. 495 pp

Freeman H, Hirose T, Schepens CL: Vitreous Surgery and Advances in Fundus Diagnosis and Treatment. New York, Appleton-Century-Crofts, 1977. 681 pp

Kanski JJ: Retinal Detachment: A Colour Manual of Diagnosis and Treatment. London, Butterworth, 1986. 161 pp

Krill A: Krill's Hereditary Retinal and Choroidal Diseases, vol 1, 2. Hagerstown, MD, Harper & Row, 1977. 1371 pp

L'Esperance Jr FA, James Jr WA: Diabetic Retinopathy. Clinical Evaluation and Management. St. Louis, Mosby, 1981. 294 pp

McPherson A (ed): New and Controversial Aspects of Vitreoretinal Surgery. St. Louis, Mosby, 1977. 455 pp

Morse P: Vitreoretinal Disease. A Manual for Diagnosis and Treatment. Chicago, Year Book Medical Publishers, 1979. 625 pp

O'Malley C, O'Malley P: The Peripheral Fundus of the Eye. New York, Medcom, 1973. 34 pp

Pruett RC, Regan CD: Retinal Congress. New York, Appleton-Century-Crofts, 1972. 730 pp

Ryan SJ, Dawson AK, Little HL (eds): Retinal Diseases. Orlando, FL, Grune & Stratton, 1985. 282 pp

Schepens CL: Retinal Detachment and Allied Diseases, vols 1, 2. Philadelphia, Saunders, 1983. 1155 pp

Sigelman J: Retinal Diseases: Pathogenesis, Laser Therapy and Surgery. Boston, Little, Brown, 1984. 442 pp

Tasman W, Shields JA: Disorders of the Peripheral Fundus. Hagerstown, MD, Harper & Row, 1980. 227 pp

Tolentino FI, Schepens CL, Freeman HM: Vitreoretinal Disorders. Diagnosis and Management. Philadelphia, Saunders, 1976. 659 pp

Transactions of the New Orleans Academy of Ophthalmology. Symposium on Retina and Retinal Surgery. St. Louis, Mosby, 1969. 406 pp

Transactions of the New Orleans Academy of Ophthalmology. Symposium on Retinal Diseases. St. Louis, Mosby, 1977. 354 pp

Wise GN, Dollery CT, Henkind P: The Retinal Circulation. New York, Harper & Row, 1971. 566 pp

Specific Bibliography

Anatomic Considerations

Allen RA, Miller DH, Straatsma BR: Cysts of the posterior ciliary body (pars plana). Arch Ophthalmol 66: 302–13, 1961

Balazs EA: Molecular morphology of the vitreous body. In Smelser GK (ed): The Structure of the Eye. New York, Academic Press, 1961, pp 293–310

Foos RY: Vitreoretinal juncture, topographical variations. Invest Ophthalmol 11:801–08, 1972

Grignolo A: Fibrous components of the vitreous body. Arch Ophthalmol 47:760–74, 1952

Grignolo A, Schepens CL, Heath P: Cysts of the pars plana ciliaris. Arch Ophthalmol 58:530–45, 1957

Hamilton AM, Taylor W: Significance of pigment granules in the vitreous. Br J Ophthalmol 56:700–02, 1972

Hogan MJ, Alvarado JA, Weddell JE: Histology of the Human Eye. Philadelphia, Saunders, 1971

Johnson BL, Storey JD: Proteinaceous cysts of the ciliary epithelium. I. Their clear nature and immunoelectrophoretic analysis in a case of multiple myeloma. II. Their occurrence in nonmyelomatous hypergammaglobulinemic conditions. Arch Ophthalmol 84:166–75, 1970

Marchesani O, Sautter H: Atlas of the Ocular Fundus. [A. Phillipp, transl.]. New York, Hafner, 1959, pp 1–26

Michaelson IC: Textbook of the Fundus of the Eye, 3rd ed. Edinburgh, Churchill Livingstone, 1980. 910 pp

Okun E: Gross and microscopic pathology in autopsy eyes. I.Introduction and long posterior ciliary nerves. Am J Ophthalmol 50:424–9, 1960

Okun E: Gross and microscopic pathology in autopsy eyes. IV. Pars plana cysts. Am J Ophthalmol 51: 1221–8, 1961

Polyak SL: The Retina. Chicago, University of Chicago Press, 1941. 607 pp

Ruiz RS: Giant cysts of the pars plana. Am J Ophthalmol 72:481–2, 1971

Rutnin U: Fundus appearance in normal eyes. I. The choroid. Am J Ophthalmol 64:821–39, 1967

Rutnin U, Schepens CL: Fundus appearance in normal eyes. II. The standard peripheral fundus and development variations. Am J Ophthalmol 64:840–52, 1967

Rutnin U, Schepens CL: Fundus appearance in normal eyes. III. Peripheral degenerations. Am j Ophthalmol 64:1040–62, 1967

Rutnin U, Schepens CL: Fundus appearance in normal eyes. IV. Retinal breaks and other findings. Am J Ophthalmol 64:1063–78, 1967

Salzmann M: The Anatomy and History of the Human Eyeball in the Normal State: Its Development and Senescence. [EVL Brown, transl.]. Chicago, University of Chicago Press, 1912

Schepens CL: Clinical aspects of pathologic changes in the vitreous body. Am J Ophthalmol 38(1, pt II):8–21, 1954

Schepens CL: Retinal Detachment and Allied Diseases, vol 1. Philadelphia, Saunders, pp 23–36, 134–61, 1983

Shafer DM: Binocular indirect ophthalmoscopy (chapter 2); General discussion: Significance of white-with-pressure. In Schepens CL, Regan CDJ (eds): Controversial Aspects of the Management of Retinal Detachment. Boston, Little, Brown, 1965, p 51

Spencer LM, Foos RY: Paravascular vitreoretinal attachments: Role in retinal tears. Arch Ophthalmol 84:557–64, 1970

Spencer LM, Foos RY, Straatsma BM: Meridional folds, meridional complexes, and associated abnormalities of the peripheral retina. Am J Ophthalmol 70:697–714, 1970

Spencer LM, Foos RY, Straatsma BR: Enclosed bays of the ora serrata: relationship to retinal tears. Arch Ophthalmol 83:421–5, 1970

Straatsma BR, Foos RY, Spender LM: The retina-topography and clinical correlations. In New Orleans Academy of

Ophthalmology: Symposium on the Retina and Retinal Surgery. St. Louis, Mosby, 1969, pp 1–26

Straatsma BR, Hall MV, Allen RA, Crescitelli F: The Retina. Los Angeles, University of California Press, 1969

Straatsma BR, Landers MB, Kreiger AE: The ora serrata in the adult human eye. Arch Ophthalmol 80:3–20, 1968

Straatsma BR, Landers MB, Kreiger AE, Apt L: Topography of the Adult Human Retina. In Straatsma BR, Hall MO, Allen RA, Crescitelli F (eds): The Retina. Morphology, Function and Clinical Characteristics. Berkeley, University of California Press, 1969, pp 379–410

Swann DA: The structure and function of the vitreous. In Pruett RC, Regan CDJ (eds): Retina Congress. New York, Appleton-Century-Crofts, 1974, pp 203–14

Swann DA, Constable IJ: Vitreous structure: II. Role of hyaluronate. Invest Ophthalmol 11:164–8, 1972

Tasman W, Shields JA: Disorders of the Peripheral Fundus. Hagerstown, MD, Harper & Row, 1980

Teng CC, Katzin KM: An anatomic study of the retina, Part I. Nonpigmented epithelium cell proliferation and hole formation. Am J Ophthalmol 34:1237–40, 1951

Thiel HL: Beitrage zur Anatomie der Ora serrata. Ber Dtsch Ophthalmol Ges 58:249–56, 1953

Thiel HL: Zur topographischen und histologischen Situation der Ora serrata. Graefes Arch Ophthalmol 156:590–629, 1955

Thiel R: Atlas of Diseases of the Eye, vol 2. [D Guerry, WJ Geeraets, H Wiesinger, transl.]. Amsterdam, Elsevier, 1963

Tolentino FJ, Schepens CL, Freeman HM: Vitreoretinal Disorders: Diagnosis and Management. Philadelphia, Saunders, 1976. 659 pp

Wolff E: Anatomy of the Eye and Orbit, 6th ed. (revised by R Warwick). Philadelphia, Saunders, 1977. 529 pp

Classification System of Peripheral Retinal Degeneration

Foos RY, Spencer LM, Straatsma BR: Trophic degenerations of the peripheral retina. In New Orleans Academy of Ophthalmology: Symposium on the Retina and Retinal Surgery. St. Louis, Mosby, 1969, pp 90–102

Spencer LM, Straatsma BR, Foos RY: Tractional degenerations of the peripheral retina. In New Orleans Academy of Ophthalmology: Symposium on the Retina and Retinal Surgery. St. Louis, Mosby, 1969, pp 103–27

Straatsma BR, Foos RY: Part II. Peripheral retinal disorders. Classification. In L'Esperance Jr FA (ed): Current Diagnosis and Management of Chorioretinal Diseases. St. Louis, Mosby, 1977, pp 97–118

Developmental Variations of the Peripheral Fundus

Ora Serrata Bays

Maggiore L: L'ora serrata nell'occhio umano. (Morfologia, sviluppo anatomia comparata e fisiologia). Ann Oftalmol Clin Ocul 52:625–723, 1924

Rutnin U, Schepens, CL: Fundus appearance in normal eyes II. The standard peripheral fundus and developmental variations. Am J Ophthalmol 64:840–52, 1967

Schepens CL: The standard peripheral fundus and its variations, In Schepens CL: Retinal Detachment and Allied Diseases, vol 1. Philadelphia, Saunders, 1983, pp 134–61

Spencer LM, Foos RY, Straatsma BR: Enclosed bays of the ora serrata. Arch Ophthalmol 83:421–5, 1970

Straatsma BR, Landers MB, Kreiger AE: The ora serrata in the adult human eye. Arch Ophthalmol 80:3–20, 1968

Dentate Processes and Meridional Folds

Eisner G: Zur spaltlampenmikroskopischer Ora serrata und Pars plana Corporis ciliaris. Graefes Arch Klin Exp Ophthalmol 177:232–47, 1969

Rutnin U, Schepens CL: Fundus appearance in normal eyes. II. The standard peripheral fundus and developmental variations. Am J Ophthalmol 64:840–52, 1967

Schepens CL: The standard peripheral fundus and its variations. In Retinal Detachment and Allied Diseases, vol 1. Philadelphia, Saunders, 1983, pp 134–61

Spencer LM, Foos RY, Straatsma BR: Meridional folds and meridional complexes of the peripheral retina. Trans Am Acad Ophthalmol Otolaryngol 73:204–21, 1969

Spencer LM, Foos RY, Straatsma BR: Enclosed bays of the ora serrata. Arch Ophthalmol 83:421–5, 1970

Spencer LM, Foos RY, Straatsma BR: Meridional folds, meridional complexes, and associated abnormalities of the peripheral retina. Am J Ophthalmol 70:697–714, 1970

Straatsma BR, Landers MB, Kreiger AE: The ora serrata in the adult human eye. Arch Ophthalmol 80:3–20, 1968

Teng CC, Katzin HM: An anatomic study of the retina. Part III: Congenital retinal rosettes. Am J Ophthalmol 36:169–85, 1953

Granular Tissue (Tags) and Zonular Traction Tufts

Byer NE: Cystic retinal tufts and their relationship to retinal detachment. Arch Ophthalmol 99:1788–90, 1981

Foos RY: Zonular traction tufts of the peripheral retina in cadaver eyes. Arch Ophthalmol 82:620–32, 1969

Foos RY: Vitreoretinal juncture: Topographical variations. Invest Ophthalmol 11:801–08, 1972

Foos R: Vitreous base, retinal tufts, and retinal tears: Pathogenic relationships. In Retina Congress. Pruett RC, Regan CDJ (eds): New York, Appleton-Century-Crofts, 1974, pp 259–280

Foos RY, Allen RA: Retinal tears and lesser lesions of the peripheral retina in autopsy eyes. Am J Ophthalmol 64:643–55, 1967

Okun E: Gross and microscopic pathology in autopsy eyes. III. Retinal breaks without detachment. Am J Ophthalmol 51:369–91, 1961

Rutnin U, Schepens CL: Fundus appearance in normal eyes. II. The standard peripheral fundus and developmental variations. Am J Ophthalmol 64:840–54, 1967

Rutnin U, Schepens CL: Fundus appearance in normal eyes. IV: Retinal breaks and other findings. Am J Ophthalmol 64:1063–78, 1967

Schepens CL: The standard peripheral fundus and its variations. In Schepens CL: Retinal Detachment and Allied Diseases, vol 1. Philadelphia, Saunders, 1983, pp 134–61

Spencer LM, Straatsma BR, Foos RY: Tractional degenerations of the peripheral retina. In New Orleans Academy of Ophthalmology: Symposium of the Retina and Retinal Surgery. St. Louis, Mosby, 1969, pp 103–27

Straatsma BR, Foos RY: Part II. Peripheral retinal disorders. Classification. In L'Esperance Jr FA (ed): Current Diagnosis and Management of Chorioretinal Diseases. St. Louis, Mosby, 1977, pp 97–118

Teng CC, Katzin HM: An anatomic study

of the periphery of the retina. Part I. Nonpigmented epithelial cell proliferation and hole formation. Am J Ophthalmol 34:1237–48, 1951

Teng CC, Katzin HM: An anatomic study of the periphery of the retina. Part III: Congenital retinal rosettes. Am J Ophthalmol 36:169–85, 1953

Ora Serrata Pearls

Lonn LI, Smith TR: Ora serrata pearls. Arch Ophthalmol 77:809–13, 1967

Rutnin U, Schepens CL: Fundus appearance in normal eyes. IV: Retinal breaks and other findings. Am J Ophthalmol 64:1063–78, 1967

Samuels B: Opacities of the vitreous. Trans Ophthalmol Soc UK 50:414, 1930

Trophic Retinal Degenerations

Vitreous Base Excavations (Retinal Erosions)

Foos RY, Allen RA: Retinal tears and lesser lesions of the peripheral retina in autopsy eyes. Am J Ophthalmol 64:643–55, 1967

Foos RY, Spencer LM, Straatsma BR: Trophic degenerations of the peripheral retina. In New Orleans Academy of Ophthalmology: Symposium on Retina and Retinal Surgery. St. Louis, Mosby, 1969, pp 90–102

Rutnin U, Schepens CL: Fundus appearance in normal eyes. III: Peripheral degenerations. Am J Ophthalmol 64(6): 1040–62, 1967

Straatsma BR, Foos RY: Part II. Peripheral Retinal Disorders. Classification. In L'Esperance Jr FA (ed): Current Diagnosis and Management of Chorioretinal Diseases. St. Louis, Mosby, 1977, pp 97–118

Retinal Holes

Foos RY, Allen RA: Retinal tears and lesser lesions of the peripheral retina in autopsy eyes. Am J Ophthalmol 64:643–55, 1967

Foos RY, Spencer LM, Straatsma BR: Trophic degenerations of the peripheral retina. In New Orleans Academy of Ophthalmology: Symposium on Retina and Retinal Surgery. St. Louis, Mosby, 1969, pp 90–102

Hanssen R: Beitrag zur Histologie des myopischen Auges, insbesondere zur Luckenbildung in der Retina und zur Entstehung der Netzhautablösung. Klin Monatsbl Augenheilkd 63:295–336, 1919

Okun E: Gross and microscopic pathology in autopsy eyes. Part III. Retinal breaks without detachment. Am J Ophthalmol 51:369–91, 1961

Rutnin V, Schepens CL: Fundus appearance in normal eyes. IV. Retinal breaks and other findings. Am J Ophthalmol 64:1063–78, 1967

Schepens CL: Retinal Detachment and Allied Diseases, vol I. Philadelphia, Saunders, 1983, pp 39, 158–60

Straatsma BR, Foos RY: Part II. Peripheral Retinal Disorders. Classification. In L'Esperance Jr FA (ed): Current Diagnosis and Management of Chorioretinal Diseases. St. Louis, Mosby, 1977, pp 97–118

Teng CC, Katzin HM: An anatomic study of the peripheral retina. II. Peripheral cystoid degeneration of the retina; Formation of cysts and holes. Am J Ophthalmol 36:29–39, 1953

Typical and Reticular Cystoid Degeneration

Foos RY, Feman SS: Reticular cystoid degeneration of the peripheral retina. Am J Ophthalmol 69:392–403, 1970

Gottinger W: Rasterelektronen mikroskopische Befunde bei peripheren cystoiden Degeneration. Dtsch Ophthalmol Ges 74:147–9, 1967

O'Malley PF, Allen RA: Peripheral cystoid degeneration of the retina. Arch Ophthalmol 77:769–76, 1967

Rutnin U, Schepens CL: Fundus appearance in normal eyes. III: Peripheral degenerations. Am J Ophthalmol 64:1040–62, 1967

Schepens CL: Retinal Detachment and Allied Diseases, vol 1. Philadelphia, Saunders, 1983, pp 141–53

Straatsma BR, Foos RY: Part II. Peripheral retinal disorders. Classification. In L'Esperance Jr FA (ed): Current Diagnosis and Management of Chorioretinal Diseases. St. Louis, Mosby, 1977, pp 97–118

Teng CC, Katzin HM: An anatomic study of the peripheral retina. II. Peripheral cystoid degeneration of the retina, formation of cysts and holes. Am J Ophthalmol 36:29–49, 1953

Acquired Typical and Reticular Degenerative Retinoschisis

Byer NE: Clinical study of senile retinoschisis. Arch Ophthalmol 79:36–44, 1986

Byer NE: The natural history of senile retinoschisis. Trans Am Acad Ophthalmol Otolaryngol 81:458–71, 1976

Foos RY: Senile retinoschisis. Relation to cystoid degeneration. Trans Am Acad Ophthalmol Otolaryngol 74:33–51, 1970

Francois J: Heredity in Ophthalmology. St. Louis, Mosby, 1961, pp 489–94

Gottinger W: Senile Retinoschisis. Stuttgart, Thieme, 1978

Hagler WS, Woldoff HS: Retinal detachment in relation to senile retinoschisis. Trans Am Acad Ophthalmol Otolaryngol 77:99–113, 1973

Hirose T, Marcil G, Schepens CL, Freeman HM: Acquired retinoschisis: Observations and treatment. In Pruett RC, Regan CDJ (eds): Retina Congress. New York, Appleton-Century-Crofts, 1972, pp 489–504

Rutnin U, Schepens CL: Fundus appearance in normal eyes. III: Peripheral degenerations. Am J Ophthalmol 64:1040–62, 1967

Schepens CL: Retinal Detachment and Allied Diseases, vol 2. Philadelphia, Saunders, 1983, pp 557–68

Shea M, Schepens CL, von Pirquet SR: I. Senile type: A clinical report of one hundred and seven cases. Arch Ophthalmol 63:1–9, 1960

Straatsma BR, Foos RY: Typical and reticular degenerative retinoschisis. Am J Ophthalmol 75:551–75, 1973

Tasman W, Shields J: Degenerative conditions. In Disorders of the Peripheral Fundus. Hagerstown, MD, Harper & Row, 1980, pp 172–6

Tolentino FI, Schepens CL, Freeman HM: Vitreoretinal Disorders: Diagnosis and Management. Philadelphia, Saunders, 1976, pp 360–5

Zimmerman LE, Spencer WH: The pathologic anatomy of retinoschisis, with a report of two cases diagnosed clinically as malignant melanoma. Arch Ophthalmol 63:10–19, 1960

Paving-Stone (Cobblestone) Degeneration

O'Malley PF, Allen RA, Straatsma BR, O'Malley CC: Paving-Stone degeneration of the retina. Arch Ophthalmol 73:169–182, 1965

Rutnin U, Schepens CL: Fundus appearance in normal eyes. III: Peripheral degenerations. Am J Ophthalmol 64: 1042–62, 1967

Schepens CL: Cobblestone degeneration of the retina. In Kimura SJ, Cagill WM (eds): Retinal Diseases. Symposium on Differential Diagnostic Problems of Posterior Uveitis. Philadelphia, Lea & Febiger, 1966, pp 195–203

Schepens CL: Retinal Detachment and Allied Diseases, vol 1. Philadelphia, Saunders, 1983, pp 154–5

Straatsma BR, Allen RA, O'Malley P, et al: Pathologic and clinical manifestations of paving stone degeneration of the retina. In McPherson A (ed): New and Controversial Aspects of Retinal Detachment. New York, Harper & Row, 1968, pp 76–99

Straatsma BR, Foos RY: Part II. Peripheral retinal disorders. Classification. In L'Esperance Jr FA (ed): Current Diagnosis and Management of Chorioretinal Diseases. St. Louis, Mosby, 1977, pp 97–118

Peripheral Tapetochoroidal (Honeycomb) Degeneration

Foos RY, Spencer LM, Straatsma BR: Trophic degenerations of the peripheral retina. In New Orleans Academy of Ophthalmology: Symposium on Retina and Retinal Surgery. St. Louis, Mosby, 1969, pp 90–102

Rutnin U, Schepens CL: Fundus appearance in normal eyes. III: Peripheral degenerations. Am J Ophthalmol 64:1042–62, 1967

Straatsma BR, Foos RY: Part II. Peripheral Retinal Disorders. Classification. In L'Esperance Jr FA (ed): Current Diagnosis and Management of Chorioretinal Diseases. St. Louis, Mosby, 1977, pp 97–118

Equatorial Drusen

Bird A: Bruch's Membrane Degenerations. I. Disciform macular degeneration. In Archer DB (ed): Krill's Hereditary Retinal and Choroidal Diseases, vol 2: Clinical Characteristics. Hagerstown, MD, Harper & Row, 1977, pp 825–49

Farkas TG, Krial AE, Sylvester VM, et al: Familial and secondary drusen: Histologic and functional correlations. Trans Am Acad Ophthalmol Otolaryngol 75:333–43, 1971

Frakas TG, Sylvester VM, Archer D, et al: The histochemistry of drusen. Am J Ophthalmol 71:1206–15, 1971

Gass JDM: Drusen and disciform macular detachment and degeneration. Arch Ophthalmol 90:206–17, 1973

Hogan MJ: Role of the retinal pigment epithelium in macular disease. Trans

Am Acad Ophthalmol Otolaryngol 76:69–80, 1972

Krill AE, Klien BA: Flecked retina syndrome. Arch Ophthalmol 4:496–508, 1965

Lonn LI, Smith TR: Ora serrata pearls. Arch Ophthalmol 77:809–13, 1967

Tasman W, Shields JA: Disorders of the Peripheral Fundus. Hagerstown, MD, Harper & Row, 1980, pp 183–5

Tractional Retinal Degenerations

Anatomic Classification of Retinal Tears

Foos RY: Tears of the peripheral retina: Pathogenesis, incidence and classification in autopsy eyes. Mod Probl Ophthalmol 15:68–81, 1975

Foos RY: Postoral peripheral retinal tears. Ann Ophthalmol 6:679–87, 1977

Sigelman J: Vitreous base classification of retinal tears: Clinical application (review). Surv Ophthalmol 25(2): 59–74, 1980

Partial-Thickness Peripheral Retinal Tears

Foos RY, Allen RA: Retinal tears and lesser lesions of the peripheral retina in autopsy eyes. Am J Ophthalmol 64:643–55, 1967

Gärtner J: Histologische Beobachtungen über physiologische vitreovasculäre Adhärenzen. Klin Monatsbl Augenheilkd 141:530, 1962

Gärtner J: Über persistierende netzhautadhärente glaskörperstränge und vitreoretinale Gefässanastomosen. Graefes Arch Ophthalmol 167:103, 1964

Rieger H: Zur Histologie der Glaskörperabhebung. II. Über die Beziehungen des abgehobenen Glaskörpers zur Netzhaut. Graefe's Arch Ophthalmol 146(4): 447–62, 1943

Rutnin U, Schepens CL: Fundus appearance in normal eyes. IV. Retinal breaks and other findings. Am J Ophthalmol 64: 1063–78, 1967

Spencer LM, Foos RY: Paravascular vitreoretinal attachments: Role in retinal tears. Arch Ophthalmol 84:557–64, 1970

Spencer LM, Straatsma BR, Foos RY: Tractional degenerations of the peripheral retina. In New Orleans Academy of Ophthalmology: Symposium of the Retina and Retinal Surgery. St. Louis, Mosby, 1969, pp 103–27

Straatsma BR, Foos RY: Part II. Peripheral retinal disorders. Classification. In L'Es-

perance Jr FA (ed): Current Diagnosis and Management of Chorioretinal Diseases. St. Louis, Mosby, 1977, pp 97–118

Full-Thickness Peripheral Retinal Tears

Arentsen JJ, Welch RB: Retinal detachment in the young individual: A survey of 100 cases seen at the Wilmer Institute. J Pediatr Ophthalmol 11:198–202, 1974

Ashrafzadeh MT, Schepens CL, Elzeneiny IT: Aphakic and phakic retinal detachment. Arch Ophthalmol 89:476–83, 1973

Benson WE, Grand MG, Okun E: Aphakic retinal detachment. Arch Ophthalmol 93:245–9, 1975

Byer NE: Clinical study of retinal breaks. Trans Am Acad Ophthalmol Otolaryngol 71:461–73, 1967

Colyear BM, Pischel DK: Clinical tears without detachment. Am J Ophthalmol 41:773–92, 1956

Cox MS, Schepens CL, Freeman HM: Retinal detachment due to ocular contusion. Arch Ophthalmol 76:678–85, 1966

Davis MD: The natural history of retinal breaks. Arch Ophthalmol 92:183–94, 1974

Delori F, Pomerantzeff O, Cox MS: Deformation of the globe under high-speed impact: Its relation to contusion injuries. Invest Ophthalmol 8:290–301, 1969

Everett WG, Katzin D: Meridional distribution of retinal breaks in aphakic retinal detachment. Am J Ophthalmol 66:928–32, 1968

Foos RY: Zonular traction tufts of the peripheral retina in cadaver eyes. Arch Ophthalmol 82:620–32, 1969

Foos RY: Posterior vitreous detachment. Trans Am Acad Ophthalmol Otolaryngol 76:480–97, 1972

Foos RY: Vitreous base, retinal tufts and retinal tears: Pathogenetic relationships. In Pruett RC, Regan CDJ (eds): Retina Congress. New York, Appleton-Century-Crofts, 1972, pp 259–80

Foos RY: Tears of the peripheral retina: Pathogenesis, incidence and classification in autopsy eyes. Mod Probl Ophthalmol 15:68–81, 1975

Foos RY: Postoral peripheral retinal tears. Ann Ophthalmol 6:679–87, 1977

Hauer Y, Barkay S: Vitreous detachment in aphakic eyes. Br J Ophthalmol 48:341–3, 1964

Heller MD, Straatsma BR, Foos RY: Detachment of the posterior vitreous in phakic and aphakic eyes. Secondary de-

tachment of the retina. Mod Probl Ophthalmol 10:23–36, 1972

Jaffe NA: Complications of acute posterior vitreous detachment. Arch Ophthalmol 79:568–71, 1968

Norton EWD: Retinal detachment in aphakia. Trans Am Ophthalmol Soc 61:770–89, 1963

Robertson DM, Curtin VT, Norton EWD: Avulsed retinal vessels with retinal breaks. Arch Ophthalmol 85:669–72, 1971

Rutnin U, Schepens CL: Fundus appearance in normal eyes. IV: Retinal breaks and other findings. Am J Ophthalmol 64:1063–78, 1967

Scheie HG, Morse PH, Aminlari A: Incidence of retinal detachment following cataract extraction. Arch Ophthalmol 89:293–5, 1973

Schepens CL: Pathogenesis of traumatic rhegmatogenous retinal detachment In Freeman HM (ed): Ocular Trauma. New York, Appleton-Century-Crofts, 1979, pp 273–84

Tasman W: Posterior vitreous detachment and peripheral retinal breaks. Trans Am Acad Ophthalmol Otolaryngol 72:217–24, 1968

Tasman W: Peripheral retinal changes following blunt trauma. Trans Am Ophthalmol Soc 70:190–8, 1972

Tasman W, Shields JA: Disorders of the peripheral fundus. Hagerstown, MD, Harper & Row, 1980, pp 205–6

Weidenthal DT, Schepens CL: Peripheral fundus changes associated with ocular contusion. Am J Ophthalmol 62:465–77, 1966

Retinal Dialyses (Juvenile)

Arentsen JJ, Welch RB: Retinal detachment in the young individual: A survey of 100 cases seen at the Wilmer Institute. J Pediatr Ophthalmol 11:198–202, 1974

Benson WE, Nantawan P, Morse PH: Characteristics and prognosis of retinal detachments with demarcation lines. Am J Ophthalmol 84:641–4, 1977

Black RK, Davies EWG: The management of retinal dialysis. Trans Ophthalmol Soc UK 87:317–33, 1967

Chignell AH: Retinal dialysis. Br J Ophthalmol 57:572–7, 1972

Cox MS: Retinal breaks caused by nonperforation trauma at the point of impact. Trans Am Ophthalmol Soc 78:413–66, 1980

Cox MS, Schepens CL, Freeman HM: Retinal detachment due to ocular contu-sion. Arch Ophthalmol 76:678–85, 1966

Duke-Elder S, Dobree JH: System of Ophthalmology, vol 10: Diseases of the Retina. London, Henry Kimpton, 1967, pp 789–90

Freeman HM, Cox MS, Schepens CL: Traumatic retinal detachments. Int Ophthalmol Clin 14(4):151–70, 1974

Hagler WS, North AW: Retinal dialyses and retinal detachment. Arch Ophthalmol 79:376–88, 1968

Hilton GF, Norton EWD: Juvenile retinal detachment. Mod Probl Ophthalmol 8:325–41, 1969

Hudson JR: Retinal detachment in children. Trans Ophthalmol Soc UK 85:79–91, 1965

Schepens CL: Pathogenesis of traumatic rhegmatogenous retinal detachment. In Freeman HM (ed): Ocular Trauma. New York, Appleton-Century-Crofts, 1979, pp 273–84

Tasman W: Peripheral retinal changes following blunt trauma. Trans Am Ophthalmol Soc 70:190–8, 1972

Tasman W: Retinal dialysis following blunt trauma. In Freeman HM (ed): Ocular Trauma. New York, Appleton-Century-Crofts, 1979, pp 295–9

Verdaguer TJ, Rojas B, Lechuga M: Genetical studies in nontraumatic retinal dialysis. Mod Probl Ophthalmol 15:34–9, 1975

Watzke RC: The ophthalmoscopic sign "white-with-pressure." Arch Ophthalmol 66:812–23, 1961

Weidenthal DT, Schepens CL: Peripheral fundus changes associated with ocular contusion. Am J Ophthalmol 62:465–77, 1966

Winslow R, Tasman W: Juvenile retinal detachment. Trans Am Acad Ophthalmol Otolaryngol 85:607–18, 1978

Giant Retinal Tears

Freeman HM: Current management of giant retinal breaks. In New Orleans Academy of Ophthalmology: Symposium on Retina and Retinal Surgery. St. Louis, Mosby, 1969, pp 171–83

Freeman HM: Current management of giant retinal breaks. In Pruett RC, Regan CDJ (eds): Retina Congress. New York, Appleton-Century-Crofts, 1972, pp 435–63

Freeman HM: Vitreous surgery. X. Current status of vitreous surgery in cases of rhegmatogenous retinal detachment. Trans Am Acad Ophthalmol Otolaryngol 77:202–15, 1973

Freeman HM: Fellow eyes of giant retinal breaks. Trans Am Ophthalmol Soc 76:343–82, 1978

Glasspool MG, Kanski JJ: Prophylaxis in giant tears. Trans Ophthalmol Soc UK 93:363–71, 1973

Hovland KR, Schepens CL, Freeman HM: Developmental giant tears associated with lens coloboma. Arch Ophthalmol 80:325–31, 1968

Kanski J: Giant retinal tears. Am J Ophthalmol 78:846–52, 1975

Lincoff HA, Kreissig I, La Franco F: Large retinal tears. Am J Ophthalmol 84:501–08, 1977

Machemer R, Allen AW: Retinal tears 180 degrees and greater. Management with vitrectomy and intravitreal gas. Arch Ophthalmol 94:1340–6, 1976

Norton EWD: Intra-ocular gas in the management of selected retinal detachments. Trans Am Acad Ophthalmol Otolaryngol 77:85–98, 1973

Norton EWD, Aaberg TM, Fung W, et al: Giant retinal tears. Am J Ophthalmol 68:1011–21, 1969

Schepens CL, Freeman HM: Current management of giant retinal breaks. Trans Am Acad Ophthalmol Otolaryngol 71:474–87, 1967

Scott JD: Equatorial giant tears affected by massive vitreous retraction. Trans Ophthalmol Soc UK 96:309–12, 1976

Scott JD: A rationale for the use of liquid silicone. Trans Ophthalmol Soc UK 97:235–7, 1977

Trophic and Tractional Retinal Degenerations

White-with- or -without-Pressure

Goldbaum MH, Joondeph N, Huamonte FU, et al: White-with-pressure or white-without-pressure lesions. In Peyman GA, Sanders DR, Goldberg MF (eds): Principles and Practice of Ophthalmology. Philadelphia, Saunders, 1980, pp 1027–8

Grignolo A: Ophthalmoscopy and other methods of examination. In Schepens CL, Regan CDJ (eds): Controversial Aspects of the Management of Retinal Detachment. Boston, Little, Brown, 1965, pp 2–28

Karlin DB, Curtin BJ: Axial length measurements and peripheral fundus changes in the myopic eye. In Pruett RC, Regan CDJ (eds): Retinal Congress. New York, Appleton-Century-Crofts, 1972, pp 629–42

Nagpal KC, Huamonte FU, Constantaras A, et al: Migratory white without pressure retinal lesions. Arch Ophthalmol 94:576–9, 1976

Rutnin U, Schepens CL: Fundus appearance in normal eyes. IV. Retinal breaks and other findings. Am J Ophthalmol 64:1063–78, 1967

Schepens CL: Subclinical retinal detachments. Arch Ophthalmol 47:593–608, 1952

Watzke RC: The ophthalmic sign white-with-pressure. A clinicopathologic correlation. Arch Ophthalmol 66:812–23, 1961

Snail-Track Retinal Degeneration

Aaberg TM, Stevens TR: Snail track degeneration of the retina. Am J Ophthalmol 73:370–6, 1972

Byer NE: Clinical study of lattice degeneration of the retina. Trans Am Acad Ophthalmol Otolaryngol 69:1064–77, 1965

Cibis PA: Vitre et décollement de rétine. Arch Ophtalmol 25:627–37, 1965

Deutman A: Vitreoretinal dystrophies. In Archer DB (ed): Krill's Hereditary Retinal and Choroidal Diseases, vol 2: Clinical Characteristics.

Gonin J: Le pathogénie du décollement spontané de la rétine. Ann Oculist 132:30, 1904

Gonin J: Le Décollement de la Rétine, Pathogénie-Traitment. Lausanne, Librairie Payot, 1934

Lattice Retinal Degeneration

Allen RA, Straatsma BR: The pathology of lattice degeneration of the retina. Mod Probl Ophthalmol 4:49–66, 1966

Byer NE: Prognosis of asymptomatic retinal breaks. Arch Ophthalmol 92:208–10, 1974

Byer NE: Changes in and prognosis of lattice degeneration of the retina, Trans Am Acad Ophthalmol Otolaryngol 78:114–25, 1974

Byer NE: A clinical definition of lattice degeneration of the retina and its variations. Mod Probl Ophthalmol 15:58–67, 1975

Byer NE: Lattice degeneration of the retina (a review). Surv Ophthalmol 23:213–48, 1979

Bonuk M, Butler FC: An autopsy study of lattice degeneration, retinal breaks and retinal pits. In McPherson A (ed): New and Controversial Aspects of Retinal Detachment. New York, Harper & Row, 1968, pp 59–75

Davis MD: Natural history of retinal breaks without detachment. Arch Ophthalmol 92:183–94, 1974

Deutman AF: Vitreoretinal dystrophies. In Archer DB (ed): Krill's Hereditary Retinal and Choroidal Diseases, vol 2: Clinical Characteristics. Hagerstown, MD, Harper & Row, 1977, pp 1093–6

Dumas J, Schepens CL: Chorioretinal lesions predisposing to retinal breaks. Am J Ophthalmol 61:620–30, 1966

Gonin J: Le Décollement de la Rétine, Pathogénie Traitement. Lausanne, Librairie Payot, 1934

Okun E: Gross and microscopic pathology in autopsy eyes. Part III. Retinal breaks without detachment. Am J Ophthalmol 51:369–91, 1961

Rutnin U, Schepens CL: Fundus appearance of normal eyes. III: Peripheral degenerations. Am J Ophthalmol 64(6):1040–62, 1967

Schepens CL: Symposium Retinal Detachment: Diagnostic and prognostic factors as found in preoperative examination. Trans Am Acad Ophthalmol Otolaryngol 56:398–418, 1952

Straatsma BR, Allen RA: Lattice degeneration of the retina. Trans Am Acad Ophthalmol Otolaryngol 66:600–12, 1962

Straatsma BR, Zeegen PD, Foos RY, et al: 30th Edward Jackson Memorial Lecture: Lattice degeneration of the retina. Trans Am Acad Ophthalmol Otolaryngol 78:87–113, 1974

Straatsma BR, Zeegen PD, Foos RY, et al: Lattice degeneration of the retina. Am J Ophthalmol 77:619–49, 1974

Streeten BW, Bert M: Retinal surface in lattice degeneration of the retina. Am J Ophthalmol 74:1201–09, 1972

Tillery WV, Lucier AC: Round atrophic holes in lattice degeneration – An important cause of phakic retinal detachment. Trans Am Ophthalmol, Otolaryngol 81:509–18, 1976

Hereditary Vitreoretinal Degenerations

Wagner's Hereditary Vitreoretinal Degeneration and Stickler's Syndrome

Alexander RL, Shea M: Wagner's disease. Arch Ophthalmol 74:310–18, 1965

Blair NP, Albert DM, Liberfarb RM, Hirose T: Hereditary progressive arthro-ophthalmopathy of Stickler. Am J Ophthalmol 88:876–88, 1979

Böhringer HR, Dieterle P, Landolt E: Zur Klinik und Pathologie der Degeneratio hyaloideo-retinalis hereditaria (Wagner). Ophthalmologica 139:330–8, 1960

Hagler WS, Crosswell HH Jr: Radial paravascular chorioretinal degeneration and retinal detachment. Trans Am Acad Ophthalmol Otolaryngol 72:203–16, 1968

Hirose T, Lee KY, Schepens CL: Wagner's hereditary vitreo-retinal degeneration and retinal detachment. Arch Ophthalmol 89:176–85, 1973

Hirose T, Miyake Y: Pigmentary paravenous chorioretinal degeneration: Fundus appearance and retinal functions. Annals of Ophthalmology 11:(5), 709–718, 1979

Jansen L: Degeneratio hyaloideo-retinalis hereditaria. Ophthalmologica 144:458–64, 1962

Knobloch WH: Inherited hyaloideo-retinopathy and skeletal dysplasia. Trans Am Ophthalmol Soc 73:417–51, 1976

Knobloch WH, Layer JM: Clefting syndromes associated with retinal detachment. Am J Ophthalmol 73:517–30, 1972

Liberfarb RM, Hirose T, Holmes LB: The Wagner-Stickler syndrome: A genetic study of twenty-two families. J Pediatr 99:394–9, 1981

Schepens CL: Retinal Detachment and Allied Diseases, vol 2. Philadelphia, Saunders, 1983, pp 599–614

Schreiner RL, McAlister WH, Marshall RE, Shearer WT: Stickler syndrome in a pedigree of Pierre Robin syndrome. Am J Dis Child 126:86–90, 1973

Stickler GB, Belau PG, Farrell FJ, et al: Hereditary progressive arthro-ophthalmopathy. Mayo Clin Proc 40:433–55, 1965

Stickler GB, Pugh DG: Hereditary progressive arthro-ophthalmopathy. II. Additional observations on vertebral abnormalities, a hearing defect and a report of a similar case. Mayo Clin Proc 42:495–500, 1967

Wagner H: Ein bisher unbekanntes Erbleiden des Auges (Degeneratio hyaloideo-retinalis hereditaria) beobachtet im Kanton Zurich. Klin Monatsbl Augenheilkd 100:840–57, 1938

Juvenile Retinoschisis

Burns RP, Lovrien FW, Cibis AB: Juvenile sex-linked retinoschisis: Clinical and genetic studies. Trans Am Acad Ophthalmol Otolaryngol 75:1011–21, 1971

Brodrick JD, Wyatt HT: Hereditary sex-linked retinoschisis. Br J Ophthalmol 57:551–9, 1973

Ede CH, Wilson RJ: Juvenile retinoschisis. Br J Ophthalmol 57:560–2, 1973

Kraushar MF, Schepens CL, Kaplan JA, Freeman HM: Congenital retinoschisis. In Bellows JG (ed): Contemporary Ophthalmology Honoring Sir Stewart Duke-Elder. Baltimore, Williams & Wilkins, 1972, pp 265–90

Lewis RA, Lee GB, Martonyi CL, et al: Familial foveal retinoschisis. Arch Ophthalmol 95:1190–6, 1977

Manschot WA: Pathology of hereditary juvenile retinoschisis. Arch Ophthalmol 88:131–8, 1972

Sabates FN: Juvenile retinoschisis. Am J Ophthalmol 62:683–8, 1966

Sarin LK, Green WR, Daile EG: Juvenile retinoschisis. Congenital vascular veils and hereditary retinoschisis. Am J Ophthalmol 57:793–6, 1964

Schepens CL: Retinal Detachment and Allied Diseases, vol 2. Philadelphia, Saunders, 1983, pp 568–88

Tasman W, Shields JA: Disorders of the Peripheral Fundus. Hagerstown, MD, Harper & Row, 1980, pp 36–41

Tolentino FI, Schepens CL, Freeman HM: Vitreoretinal Disorders: Diagnosis and Management. Philadelphia, Saunders, 1976, pp 249–59

Yanoff M, Rahn EK, Zimmerman LE: Histopathology of juvenile retinoschisis. Arch Ophthalmol 79:49–53, 1968

Zimmerman LE, Naumann G: The pathology of retinoschisis. In McPherson A (ed): New and Controversial Aspects of Retinal Detachment. New York, Hoeber / Harper & Row, 1968, pp 400–23

Goldman-Favre Disease

Blanck MF, Polliot L, Bernard P: La dégénérescence hyaloide tapéto-rétinienne de Goldmann et Favré à propos d'un cas. Bull Mem Soc Fr Ophtal 86:242–5, 1973

Carr RE, Siegel JM: The vitreo-tapeto-retinal degenerations. Arch Ophthalmol 84:436–45, 1970

Deutman AF: Vitreoretinal dystrophies. In Archer DB (ed): Krill's Hereditary Retinal and Choroidal Diseases, vol 2: Clinical Characteristics. Hagerstown, MD, Harper & Row, 1977, pp 1062–8

Favre M, Goldmann H: Zur Genese der hinteren Glaskörperabhebung. Ophthalmologica 132:87–97, 1957

Favre M: A propos de deux cas de dégénérescence hyaloidéo-rétinienne. Ophthalmologica. 135:604–09, 1958

Feiler-Ofry V, Adams A, Regenbogen L: Hereditary vitreoretinal degeneration and night blindness. Am J Ophthalmol 67:553–8, 1969

Francois J, de Rouck A, Cambie E: Dégénérescence hyaloidéo-tapéto-rétinienne de Goldmann-Favre. Ophthalmologica 168:81–96, 1974

Gerhard JP, Bronner A, Flament J: Rétinopathie pigmentaire et décollement de la rétine. Bull Soc Ophtalmol Fr 72:133–6, 1972

Goldmann H: Biomicroscopic du corps vitré et du fond d'œil. Rapp Soc Fr Ophtalmol, pp 164–9, 1957

Ricci A: Clinique et transmission héréditaire des dégénérescences vitréo-rétiniennes. Bull Soc Ophtalmol Fr 61:618–62, 1961

Stankovic I, Kecmanovic Z, Drincic V: Contribution à la connaissance de l'hérédité de la dégénérescence hyaloidéo-tapéto-rétinienne de Favre-Goldmann. Bull Mem Soc Fr Ophtalmol 86:246–50, 1973

Familial Exudative Vitreoretinopathy

Criswick VG, Schepens CL: Familial exudative vitreoretinopathy. Am J Ophthalmol 68:578–94, 1969

Deutman AF: Vitreoretinal dystrophies. In Archer DB (ed): Krill's Hereditary Retinal and Choroidal Diseases, vol 2: Clinical Characteristics. Hagerstown, MD, Harper & Row, 1977, pp 1084–92

Gow J, Oliver GL: Familial exudative vitreoretinopathy. An expanded view. Am J Ophthalmol 86:150–5, 1971

Snowflake Degeneration

Deutman AF: Vitreoretinal dystrophies. In Archer DB (ed): Krill's Hereditary Retinal and Choroidal Diseases. Hagerstown, MD, Harper & Row, 1977, pp 1097–1100

Hirose T, Lee KY, Schepens CL: Snowflake degeneration in hereditary vitreoretinal degeneration. Am J Ophthalmol 77:143–53, 1974

Hirose T, Wolf E, Schepens CL: Retinal functions in snowflake degeneration. Ann Ophthalmol 12:1135–46, 1980

Schepens CL: Retinal Detachment and Allied Diseases, vol 2. Philadelphia, Saunders, 1983, pp 614–15

Systemic Conditions Associated with Vitreoretinal Degeneration

Marfan's Syndrome

Archard C: Arachnodactylie. Bull Mem Soc Med Hop Paris 19:834–40, 1902

Franceschetti A, Francois J, Babel J: Les Hérédodégénérescences Choriorétiniennes (Dégénérescences Tapeto-Rétiniennes), vol 1, 2. Paris, Masson, 1963

Heilmann K, Suschke J, Murken JD: Marfan-Syndrome. Ophthalmologische, klinische, biochemische und genetische Untersuchungen. Ber. 70. Bericht über die Zusammenkunft der Deutschen Ophthalmologischen Gesellschaft, Heidelberg, 1969. München, Bergmann, 1970, pp 457, 599

Lloyd RI: The clinical course of the eye complications of arachrodactylia. Trans Am Ophthalmol Soc 45:342, 1947

Marfan B: Un cas de déformation congénitale des quatre membres, plus prononcée aux extrémités, caractérisée par l'allongement des os avec un certain degré d'amincissement. Bull Med Soc Hop Paris 13:220–6, 1896

Schepens CL: Retinal Detachment and Allied Diseases, vol 1. Philadelphia, Saunders, 1983, pp 268–70

Sinclair RJG, Kitchin AW, Turner RWD: The Marfan Syndrome. Q J Med 29:19–46, 1960

Homocystinuria

Allen RA, Straatsma BR, Apt L, Hall MO: Ocular manifestations of Marfan's syndrome. Trans Am Acad Ophthalmol Otolaryngol 71:18–38, 1967

Carson NAJ, Dent CE, Field CMB, Gaull CE: Homocystinuria: Clinical and pathological review of ten cases. J Pediat 6:565–83, 1965

Cross HE, Jensen AD: Ocular manifestations in Marfan's syndrome and homocystinuria. Am J Ophthalmol 75:405–20, 1973

Field CMB, Carson NAJ, Cosworth DC, et al: Homocystinuria: A new disorder of metabolism. 10th International Congress of Pediatrics, Lisbon, 1962, p 274

Francois J, Gaudier B, Pruvot J: La rétine dans l'homocystinurie. Bull Soc Ophtalmol Fr 68:582–4, 1968

Francois J: Ocular manifestations in amino-acidopathies. Adv Ophthalmol 25:28, 1972

Henkind P, Ashton N: Ocular pathology in homocystinuria. Trans Ophthalmol Soc UK 85:21–38, 1965

Hudson JR: Marfan's syndrome with retinal detachment. Br J Ophthalmol 35:244–5, 1951

Lieberman TN, Podos SM, Hartstein J: Acute glaucoma, ectopia lentis, and homocystinuria. Am J Ophthalmol 61:252–5, 1966

Schmike RN, McKusick VA, Huang T, Pollack AD: Homocystinuria studies of twenty families with thirty-eight affected members. JAMA 193:711–19, 1965

Spaeth GL, Barber GW: Homocystinuria, its ocular manifestation. J Pediat Ophthalmol 3:42–8, 1966

Ehlers-Danlos Syndrome

Beighton P: X-linked inheritance in the Ehlers-Danlos syndrome. Br Med J 2:409–11, 1968

Beighton P: Serious ophthalmological complications in the Ehlers-Danlos syndrome. Br J Ophthalmol 54:263–8, 1970

Bossu A, Lambrechts J: Manifestations oculaires du syndrome d'Ehlers-Danlos. Ann Oculist (Paris) 187:227–36, 1954

Cottini GB: Concurrence of the Groenblad-Strandberg syndrome and the Ehlers-Danlos syndrome. Acta Derm 29:544–9, 1949

Danlos H: Un cas de cutis laxa avec tumeurs par contusion chromique des coudes et des genoux. Bull Soc Fr Derm Syphilo 19:70, 1908

Durham DG: Cutis hyperelastica (Ehlers-Danlos syndrome) with blue scleras, microcornea, and glaucoma. Arch Ophthalmol 49:220–1, 1953

Ehlers E: Cutis laxa. Neigung zu Hamorrhagien in der Haut, Lockerung mehrerer Artikulationen. Dermatol Wochenschr 8:173, 1899

Green WR: Angioid streaks in Ehlers-Danlos syndrome. Arch Ophthalmol 76:197, 1966

Jansen LH: The structure of the connective tissue, an explanation of the symptoms and Ehlers-Danlos syndrome. Dermatologica 110:108–20, 1955

Johnson SAM, Falls HF: Ehlers-Danlos syndrome: A clinical and genetic study. Arch Dermatol Syphilol 60:80–105, 1949

Méténier P: A propos d'un familial de maladie d'Ehlers-Danlos. Thesis. University of Algiers, 1939, p 55

Pemberton JW, Freeman HM, Schepens CL: Familial retinal detachment and the Ehlers-Danlos syndrome. Arch Ophthalmol 76:817–24, 1966

Summer GK: The Ehlers-Danlos syndrome: A review of the literature and report of a case with subgaleal hematoma and Bell's palsy. Am J Dis Child 91:419–28, 1956

Wiedermann HR: Einiges zum Syndrom von Ehlers and Danlos. Z Kinderheilkd 100:252–6, 1952

Degenerative Conditions of the Vitreous Body

Asteroid Hyalosis

Agarwal IP, Mohan M, Khosla PK, Gupta AK: Synchysis scintillians or asteroid bodies. Orient Arch Ophthalmol 1:167–70, 1963

Bard LA: Asteroid hyalitis: Relationship to diabetes and hypercholesterolemia. Am J Ophthalmol 58:239–42, 1964

Benson AH: A case of "monocular asteroid hyalitis." Trans Ophthalmol Soc UK 14:101–04, 1894

Cibis P: Vitreoretinal Pathology and Surgery in Retinal Detachment. St. Louis, Mosby, 1965, p 193

Duke-Elder WS: System of Ophthalmology, vol 11. Diseases of the Lens and the Vitreous; Glaucoma and Hypotony. London, Henry Kimpton, 1969, pp 323–8

Hatfield RE, Gastineau CF, Rucker CW: Asteroid bodies in the vitreous: Relationship to diabetes and hypercholesterolemia. Proc Mayo Clin 37:513–14, 1962

Hogan M, Zimmerman L: Ophthalmic Pathology. An Atlas and Textbook, 2nd ed. Philadelphia, Saunders, 1962, pp 62, 651

Luxemberg M, Sime D: Relationship of asteroid hyalosis to diabetes mellitus and plasma lipid levels. Am J Ophthalmol 67:406–13, 1969

March W, Shock D, O'Grady R: Composition of asteroid bodies. Invest Ophthalmol 13:701–05, 1974

Pau H: Ätiologische Betrachtungen zur Scintallatio Nivea. Ophthalmologica (Basel) 150:167–74, 1965

Rodman HI, Johnson FB, Zimmerman LE: New histopathological and histochemical observations concerning asteroid hyalitis. Arch Ophthalmol 66:552–63, 1961

Rutherford CW: Asteroid bodies in the vitreous. Arch Ophthalmol 9:106–17, 1933

Smith JL: Asteroid hyalitis: Incidence of diabetes mellitus and hypercholesterolemia. JAMA 168:891–3, 1958

VerHoeff FH: Microscopic findings in a case of asteroid hyalitis. Am J Ophthalmol 4:155–60, 1921

Synchysis Scintillans

Forsius H: Cholesterol crystals in the anterior chamber. Acta Ophthalmol 39:284–301, 1961

Hughes WL, in discussion, Bonaccalto G: Synchysis scintillans in the anterior chamber. Arch Ophthalmol 18:477, 1937

Jaffe NS: The Vitreous in Clinical Ophthalmology. St. Louis, Mosby, 1969, pp 223–6

Koby FE: Biomicroscopie du Corps Vitré. Paris, Masson, 1932, p 100

Manschot WA: Synchysis scintillans. Acta Ophthalmol 20:80–90, 1942

Michiels J, Garin P: Synchisis étincelant de la chambre antérieure. Bull Soc Belg Ophtalmol 151:455–63, 1969

Valenin F: Über die fettähnlichen Substanzen im Glasskörper des Pferdeauges. Z Physiol Chem 105:33–57, 1919

Wand M, Gorn RA: Cholesterolosis of the anterior chamber. Am J Ophthal 78:143–4, 1974

Primary Hereditary Familial Amyloidosis

Andersson R, Kassman T: Vitreous opacities in primary familial amyloidosis. Acta Ophthalmol 46:441–7, 1968

Cohen AS: Amyloidosis. N Engl J Med 277:(10)522–630; (11)574–583; (12)628–638, 1967

Crawford JB: Cotton wool exudates in systemic amyloidosis. Arch Ophthalmol 78:214–16, 1967

Cupper C: Augenbefunde bei Paramyloid. Ber Dtsch Ophthalmol Ges 56:337–9, 1951

Falls HF, Jackson J, Carey J, et al: Ocular manifestations of hereditary primary systemic amyloidosis. Arch Ophthalmol 54:660–4, 1958

Ferry AP, Lieberman TW: Bilateral amyloidosis of the vitreous body. Report of a case without systemic or familial involvement. Arch Ophthalmol 94:982–91, 1976

Franceschetti AT, Rubinowicz T: Les lésions oculaires dans l'amyloidose primaire familiale. J Genet Hum 17: 349–66, 1969

Kantarjian AD, DeJong R: Familial primary amyloidosis with nervous system involvement. Neurology 3:399–409, 1953

Kaufman HE: Primary familial

amyloidosis. Arch Ophthalmol 60:1036–43, 1959

Kaufman HE, Thomas LB: Vitreous opacities diagnostic of familial primary amyloidosis. N Engl J Med 261:1267–71, 1959

Missmahl HP, Siebner H: Chromosomen-untersuchung bei familiarer perikollagener Amyloidose. Dtsch Med Wochenschr 90:1002–4, 1965

Paton D, Duke JR: Primary familial amyloidosis. Am J Ophthalmol 61:736–47, 1966

Rukavina JG, Block WD, Jackson C, et al: Primary systemic amyloidosis: A review and an experimental, genetic, and clinical study of twenty-nine cases with particular emphasis on familial form. Medicine 35:239–334, 1956

Wong VG, McFarlin DE: Primary familial amyloidosis. Arch Ophthalmol 78:208–13, 1967

Proliferative Retinopathies

Diabetic Retinopathy

Aaberg TM: Clinical results in vitrectomy for diabetic traction retinal detachment. Am J Ophthalmol 88:246–53, 1979

Aiello LM, Beetham WP, Balodimos MC, et al: Ruby laser photocoagulation in treatment of diabetes proliferating retinopathy: Primary report. In Goldberg M, Fine S (eds): Symposium on the Treatment of Diabetic Retinopathy. Washington, DC, US Department of Health, Education, and Welfare, Public Health Service Publication No. 1890, US Government Printing Office, 1969, pp 437–63.

Benson WE, Spalter HF: Vitreous hemorrhage. A review of experimental and clinical investigations. Surv Ophthalmol 15:297–311, 1971

Benson WE, Tasman W, Duane TD: Diabetic retinopathy. In Duane TD (ed): Clinical Ophthalmology, vol III. Hagerstown, MD, Harper & Row, 1976, pp 1–24

Blankenship G: Pars plana vitrectomy for diabetic retinopathy. A report of eight years experience. Mod Probl Ophthalmol 20:376–86, 1979

Blankenship GW, Skyler JS: Diabetic retinopathy. A general survey. Diabetes Care 1:127–31, 1978

Bresnick GH, Davis MD, Myers FL, et al: Clinical pathologic correlations in diabetic retinopathy. II. Clinical and histologic appearances of retinal capillary microaneurysms. Arch Ophthal 95:1215–1220, 1977

Brotherman DP: Diabetic retinopathy. A perspective. Surv Ophthalmol 16:359–70, 1972

Burditt AF, Caird FL, Draper GJ: The natural history of diabetic retinopathy. Q J Med 37:303–17, 1968

Caird FI, Pirie A, Ramsell TG: Diabetes and the Eye. Oxford and Edinburgh, Blackwell Scientific Publications, 1968, pp 1–7

Cogan DG, Toussaint D, Kuwabara T: Retinal vascular patterns. IV. Diabetic retinopathy. Arch Ophthalmol 66:366–78, 1961

Cogan DG, Kuwabara T: Ocular microangiopathy in diabetes. In Kimura JS, Caygill WM (eds): Vascular Complications of Diabetes Mellitus. St. Louis, Mosby, 1967, pp 53–73

Davis MD: Vitreous contraction in proliferative diabetic retinopathy. Arch Ophthalmol 74:741–51, 1965

The Diabetic Retinopathy Study Research Group: Preliminary report on effects of photocoagulation therapy. Am J Ophthalmol 81:383–6, 1976

The Diabetic Retinopathy Study Research Group: Photocoagulation treatment of diabetic retinopathy: The second report of diabetic retinopathy study findings. Ophthalmology 85:82–105, 1978

The Diabetic Retinopathy Study Research Group: Four risk factors for severe visual loss in diabetic retinopathy: The third report from the diabetic retinopathy study. Arch Ophthalmol 97:654–5, 1979

The Diabetic Retinopathy Study Research Group: Protocoagulation of proliferative diabetic retinopathy: Clinical application of diabetic retinopathy study (DRS) findings. Ophthalmology 88:583–600, 1981

Dobree JH: Proliferative diabetic retinopathy. Evolution of the retinal lesions. Br J Ophthalmol 48:637–49, 1964

Irvine AR, Norton EWD: Photocoagulation for diabetic retinopathy. Am J Ophthalmol 71:437–45, 1971

Kahn HA, Bradely RF: Prevalence of diabetic retinopathy. Br J Ophthalmol 59:345–49, 1979

Keen H: The prevalence of blindness in diabetes. J R Coll Physicians London 7:53–61, 1972

Knowler WC, Bennett PH, Ballintine EJ: Increased incidence of retinopathy in diabetics with elevated blood pressure. N Engl J Med 302:645–50, 1980

Kohner EM: The evolution and natural history of diabetic retinopathy. Int Ophthalmol Clin 18:1–16, 1978

L'Esperance Jr FA, James Jr WA: Diabetic Retinopathy. Clinicial Evaluation and Management. St. Louis, Mosby, 1981, pp 89–114

Little HL: Pathogenesis. In L'Esperance FA Jr, James WA Jr (eds): Diabetic Retinopathy. Clinical Evaluation and Management. St. Louis, Mosby, 1981, pp 58–88

Mandelcorn MS, Blankenship G, Machemer R: Pars plana vitrectomy for the management of severe diabetic retinopathy. Am J Ophthalmol 81:561–70, 1976

McMeel JW: Diabetic retinopathy: Fibrotic proliferation and retinal detachment. Trans Am Ophthalmol Soc 69:440–93, 1971

Michels RG: Vitrectomy for complications of diabetic retinopathy. Arch Ophthalmol 96:237–46, 1978

Morse PH, Aminlari A, Scheie HG: Spontaneous vitreous hemorrhage. Arch Ophthalmol 92:297–8, 1974

Patz A, Schatz H, Berkow JW, et al: Macular edema – an overlooked complication of diabetic retinopathy. Trans Am Acad Ophthalmol Otolaryngol 77:34–42, 1973

Schatz H, Patz A: Cystoid maculopathy in diabetics. Arch Ophthalmol 94:761–8, 1976

Sigelman J: Diabetic maculopathy. In L'Esperance FA Jr, James WA Jr (eds): Diabetic Retinopathy. Clinical Evaluation and Management. St. Louis, Mosby, 1981, pp 191–201

Spalter HF: Photocoagulation of diabetic retinopathy. (A rationale). In Goldberg M, Fine S (eds): Symposium on the Treatment of Diabetic Retinopathy. Washington, DC, US Department of Health, Education, and Welfare, Public Health Service No. 1890, US Government Printing Office, 1969, pp 545–53

Spalter HF: Photocoagulation of circinate maculopathy in diabetic retinopathy. Am J Ophthalmol 71:242–50, 1971

Tasman W: Retinal detachment secondary to proliferative diabetic retinopathy. Arch Ophthalmol 87:286–9, 1972

Tolentino FI, Lee PF, Schepens CL: Biomicroscopic study of vitreous cavity in diabetic retinopathy. Arch Ophthalmol 75:238–46, 1966

Retinal Vein Occlusion

Blankenship GW, Okun E: Retinal tributary vein occlusions. Arch Ophthalmol 89:363–8, 1973

Campbell CJ, Wise GN: Photocoagulation therapy of branch vein obstructions. Am J Ophthalmol 75:28–31, 1973

Chester EM: Central retinal vein occlusion. In The Ocular Fundus In Systemic Disease. Chicago, Year Book Medical Publishers, 1973, pp 116–19

Fujino T, Curtin VT, Norton EW: Experimental central retinal vein occlusion: A comparison of intraocular and extraocular occlusions. Trans Am Ophthalmol Soc 66:318–78, 1968

Gutman FA: Macular edema in branch retinal vein occlusion: Prognosis and management. Trans Am Acad Ophthalmol Otolaryngol 83:488–93, 1977

Gutman FA, Zegarra H: The natural course of temporal retinal branch vein occlusion. Trans Am Acad Ophthalmol Otolaryngol 78:178–92, 1974

Gutman FA, Zegarra H, Raver A, et al: Photocoagulation in retinal branch vein occlusion. Ann Ophthalmol 13:1359–63, 1981

Hayreh SS: Occlusion of the central retinal vessels. Br J Ophthalmol 49:626–45, 1965

Jaeger EA: Venous obstructive disease of the retina. In Duane TD (ed): Clinical Ophthalmology, vol 3. Hagerstown, MD, Harper & Row, 1978, pp 1–13

Jensen VA: Clinical studies of tributary thrombosis in the central retinal vein. Acta Ophthalmol (Suppl) 10:1–193, 1936

Kelley JS, Patz A, Schatz H: Management of retinal vein occlusion: The role of argon laser photocoagulation. Ann Ophthalmol 6:1123–34, 1974

Koyanagi Y: Die Bedeutung der Gefässkreuzung für die Entstehung der Astthrombose der retinalen Zentralvene. Klin Monatsbl Augenheilkd 81:219–31, 1928

Michels RG, Gass JDM: The natural course of retinal branch vein obstruction. Trans Am Acad Ophthalmol Otolaryngol 78:166–77, 1974

Orth DH, Patz A: Retinal branch vein occlusion. Surv Ophthalmol 22:357–76, 1978

Paton A, Rubinstein K, Smith VH: Arterial insufficiency in retinal venous occlusion. Trans Ophthalmol Soc UK 84:559–95, 1964

Rabinowicz IM, Litman S, Michaelson IC: Branch venous thrombosis: A pathological report. Trans Ophthalmol Soc UK 88:191–210, 1968

Rosen E: Fluorescein Photography of the Eye. New York, Appleton-Century-Crofts, 1969, pp 212–26

Seitz R: The Retinal Vessels: Comparative Ophthalmoscopic and Histologic Studies on Health and Diseased Eyes. St. Louis, Mosby 1964, pp 75–101

Wetzig PC: The treatment of acute branch vein occlusion by photocoagulation. Am J Ophthalmol 87:65–73, 1979

Wise GN, Dollery CT, Henkind P: Central vein occlusion. In The Retinal Circulation. New York, Harper & Row, 1971, pp 351–64

Sickle Cell Retinopathy

Edington GM, Sarkies JWR: Two cases of sickle cell anemia associated with retinal microaneurysms. Trans R Soc Trop Med Hyg 46:59–62, 1952

Goldberg MF: Natural history of untreated proliferative sickle retinopathy. Arch Ophthalmol 85:428–37, 1971

Goldberg MF: Treatment of proliferative sickle retinopathy. Trans Am Acad Ophthalmol Otolaryngol 75:532–56, 1971

Goldberg MF: Classification and pathogenesis of proliferative sickle retinopathy. Ophthalmology 71:649–65, 1971

Goldberg MF: Sickle cell retinopathy. In Duane TD (ed): Clinical Ophthalmology, vol 3. Hagerstown, MD, Harper & Row. 1976, pp 1–45

Goldberg MF: Classification and pathogenesis of proliferative sickle retinopathy. Am J Ophthalmol 71:649–65, 1971

Goldberg M, Charache S, Acacio I: Ophthalmologic manifestations of sickle cell thalassemia. Arch Intern Med 128:33–9, 1971

Goodman G, von Sallman L, Holland MG: Ocular manifestations of sickle-cell disease. Arch Ophthalmol 58:655–82, 1957

Hannon JF: Vitreous hemorrhage: Associated with sickle cell hemoglobin C disease. Am J Ophthalmol 42:707–12, 1956

Henry MD, Chapman AZ: Vitreous hemorrhage and retinopathy associated with sickle-cell disease. Am J Ophthalmol 38:204–9, 1954

Isbey EI, Tanaka KR, Clifford GO: Vitreous hemorrhage: Associated with sickle-cell trait and sickle-cell hemoglobin C disease. Am J Ophthalmol 45:870–9, 1958
Jampol LM, Goldbaum MH: Peripheral proliferative retinopathies. Surv Ophthalmol 25:1–14, 1980

Kennedy JJ, Cope CB: Intraocular lesions associated with sickle cell disease. Arch Ophthalmol 58:163–8, 1957

Lieb WA, Geeraets WJ, Guerry D III: Sickle-cell retinopathy. Acta Ophthalmol (Suppl) 58:1–45, 1959

Nagpal KC, Goldberg MF, Rabb MF: Ocular manifestations of sickle hemoglobinopathies: Surv Ophthalmol 21:391–411, 1977

Patton D: Angioid streaks and sickle cell anemia. Arch Ophthalmol 62:852–8, 1959

Romayananda N, Goldberg MF, Green WR: Histopathology of sickle cell retinopathy. Trans Am Acad Ophthalmol Otolaryngol 77:652–76, 1973

Rudd C, Evans PJ, Peeney ALP: Ocular complications in thalassemia minor. Br J Ophthalmol 37:353–8, 1953

Welch RB, Goldberg MF: Sickle-cell hemoglobin and its relation to fundus abnormality. Arch Ophthalmol 75:353–62, 1966

Retrolental Fibroplasia

Ashton N, Gardner A, Knight G: Intermittent oxygen in retrolental fibroplasia. Am J Ophthalmol 71:153–60, 1971

Ashton N, Graymore C, Pedler C: Studies on developing retinal vessels. V. Mechanism of vaso-obliteration. Br J Ophthalmol 41:449–60, 1957

Ashton N, Ward B, Serpell G: Effect of oxygen on developing retinal vessels with particular reference to the problem of retrolental fibroplasia. Br J Ophthalmol 38:397–432, 1954

Faris BM, Brockhurst RJ: Retrolental fibroplasia in the cicatricial stage. Arch Ophthalmol 82:60–5, 1969

Flynn JT, Cassady J, Essner D, et al: Fluorescein angiography in retrolental fibroplasia: Experience from 1969–1977. Ophthalmol 86: 1700–23, 1979

Friedenwald JS, Owens WC, Owens EU: Retrolental fibroplasia in premature infants. III. Pathology of the disease. Trans Am Ophthalmol Soc 49:207–34, 1951

Huggert A: Appearance of the fundus oculi in prematurely born infants treated with and without oxygen. Acta Paediatr (Uppsala) 43:327–36, 1954

King MJ: Retrolental fibroplasia: A clinical study of two hundred and thirty-eight

cases. Arch Ophthalmol 43:694–711, 1950

Kingham JD: Acute retrolental fibroplasia. Arch Ophthalmol 95:39–47, 1977

Masaryk J: Fibroplasia in the vitreous. Ann Ophthalmol 4:40–6, 1972

McPherson AR, Wittner HM, Kretzer FL: Retinopathy of Prematurity: Current concepts and Controversies. Toronto, B.C. Deckner, 1986, 237 pp

Michelson PE, Patz A, Howell R: Oxygen studies in retrolental fibroplasia. Ann Ophthalmol 27:73–8, 1970

Patz A: Clinical and experimental studies on role of oxygen in retrolental fibroplasia. Trans Am Acad Ophthalmol Otolaryngol 58:45–50, 1954

Patz A: Oxygen studies in retrolental fibroplasia. IV. Clinical and experimental observations. Am J Ophthalmol 38:291–308, 1954

Patz A: Retrolental fibroplasia. Surv Ophthalmol 14:1–29, 1969

Patz A, Eastham A, Higginbotham D, Kleh T: Oxygen studies in retrolental fibroplasia: Production of microscopic changes of retrolental fibroplasia in experimental animals. Am J Ophthalmol 36:1511–22, 1953

Patz, A, Hoeck LE, De La Cruz E: Studies on effect of high oxygen administration in retrolental fibroplasia: Nursery observations. Am J Ophthalmol 35: 1248–53, 1952

Reese AB: Persistence and hyperplasia of primary vitreous: Retrolental fibroplasia –Two entities. Arch Ophthalmol 41:527–52, 1949

Reese AB, Blodi FC: Retrolental fibroplasia. Am J Ophthalmol 34:1–24, 1951

Reese AB, Payne R: Persistence and hyperplasia of the primary vitreous, tunica vasculosa lentis or retrolental fibroplasia. Trans Am Ophthalmol Soc 43:163–92, 1945

Reese AB, Stepanik J: Cicatricial stage of retrolental fibroplasia. Am J Ophthalmol 38:308–16, 1954

Tasman W: Late complications of retrolental fibroplasia. Ophthalmology 86:1724–40, 1979

Tasman W, Annesley W: Retinal detachment in the retinopathy of prematurity. Arch Ophthalmol 75:608–14, 1966

Terry TL: Extreme prematurity and fibroblastic overgrowth of persistent vascular sheath behind each crystalline lens. I. Preliminary report. Am J Ophthalmol 25:203–4, 1942

Terry TL: Fibroblastic overgrowth of persistent tunica vasculosa lentis in premature infants. II. Report of cases – Clinical aspects. Arch Ophthalmol 29:36–53, 1943

Tolentino FI, Schepens CL, Freeman HM: Vitreoretinal Disorders. Philadelphia, Saunders, 1976, pp 207–25

Zacharias L: Retrolental fibroplasia. J Pediatr 64:156–8, 1964

Inflammatory Disorders

Sarcoidosis

Chumbley LC, Kearns TP: Retinopathy of sarcoidosis. Am J Ophthalmol 73:123–31, 1972

Crick RP: Ocular sarcoidosis. Trans Ophthalmol Soc UK 75:189–206, 1955

Cross AG: Ocular sarcoidosis. Trans Ophthalmol Soc UK 75:181–7, 1955

Ferguson RH, Paris J: Sarcoidosis: Study of twenty-nine cases with a review of splenic, hepatic, mucous membrane, retinal and joint manifestations. Arch Intern Med 101:1065, 1958

Fine M, Flocks M: Bilateral acute neuroretinitis with sarcoidosis treated with cortisporin and cortisone. Arch Ophthalmol 50:358–62, 1953

Franceschetti A, Babel J: La choriorétinite en "taches de bougie" manifestation de la maladie de Besnier-Boeck. Ophthalmologica 118:701, 1949

Geeraets WJ, McNeer KW, Maxey EF, Guerry III D: Retinopathy in sarcoidosis. Acta Ophthalmol 40:492–514, 1962

Goldberg S, Newell FW: Sarcoidosis with retinal involvement. Arch Ophthalmol 32:93–6, 1944

Gould HL, Kaufman HE: Boeck's sarcoid of the ocular fundus. Am J Ophthalmol 52:633–7, 1961

Gould HL, Kaufman HE: Sarcoid of the fundus. Arch Ophthalmol 65:453–6, 1961

James DG, Anderson R, Langley DA, et al: Ocular sarcoidosis. Br J Ophthalmol 46:461–70, 1964

James DG, Neville E, Langley DA: Ocular sarcoidosis. Trans Ophthalmol Soc UK 96:133–9, 1976

Landers PN: Vitreous lesions observed in Boeck's sarcoid. Am J Ophthalmol 32:1740–1, 1949

Letocha CE, Shields JA, Goldberg RE: Retinal changes in sarcoidosis. Can J Ophthalmol 10:184–92, 1975

Levitt JM: Boeck's sarcoid with ocular localization. Arch Ophthalmol 26:358–88, 1941

MacDonald A: Boeck's sarcoid of the retina-miliary form. Trans Am Ophthalmol Soc 41:200, 1943

Maumenee AE, Zimmerman LE: Ocular aspects of sarcoidosis. Am Rev Respir Dis 84(5)Pt 2:38–44, 1961

Obenauf CD, Shaw HE, Snydor CF, Klintworth GK: Sarcoidosis and its ophthalmic manifestations. Am J Ophthalmol 86:648–55, 1978

Ohno S, Matsuda H: Association between HLA and endogenous uveitis. In Acta: Henkind P (ed): 24th International Congress of Ophthalmology. Philadelphia, Lippincott, 1982, pp 558–60

Harada's Syndrome
(Vogt-Koyanagi-Harada's Syndrome)

Harada Y: (A clinical study of nonsupportive choroiditis (acute diffuse choroiditis). Nippon Ganka Gakkai Zasshi (Acta Soc Ophthalmol Jpn) 30:356–78, 1926

Koyanagi Y: Dysakosis, Alopecia und Poliosisbei Schwerer Uveitis nicht traumatischen Ursprungs. Klin Monatsbl Augenheilkd 82:194–211, 1929

Ohno S, Char DH, Kimura SJ, O'Connor GR: Vogt-Koyanagi-Harada syndrome. Am J Ophthalmol 83: 735–40, 1977

Pattison EM: Uveomeningoencephalitic syndrome (Vogt-Koyanagi-Harada). Arch Neurol 12:197–205, 1965

Perry HD, Font RL: Clinical and histopathologic observations in severe Vogt-Koyanagi-Harada syndrome. Am J Ophthalmol 83:242–54, 1977

Rogell G: Infections and inflammatory diseases. In Duane TD(ed): Clinical Ophthalmology, vol 3. Philadelphia, Harper & Row, 1981, pp 1–24

Shimizu K: Harada's, Behcet's, Vogt-Koyanagi syndromes: Are they clinical entities? Trans Am Acad Ophthalmol Otolaryngol 77:281–90, 1973

Suguira S: Vogt-Koyanagi-Harada disease. Jpn J Ophthalmol 22:9–35, 1978

Synder DA, Tessler HH: Vogt-Koyanagi-Harada syndrome. Am J Ophthalmol 90:69–75, 1980

Yoshioka H: Fluorescence fundus angiographic findings in early stages of Harada's syndrome. Acta Soc Ophthalmol Jpn 72:2298–306, 1968

Pars Planitis (Peripheral Uveitis)

Aaberg TM, Cesarz TJ, Flinkinger RR: Treatment of peripheral uveoretinitis by

cryotherapy. Am J Ophthalmol 73:685–8, 1973

Brockhurst RJ, Schepens CL, Okamura ID: Uveitis I. Gonioscopy. Am J Ophthalmol 42: 545–54, 1956

Brockhurst RJ, Schepens CL, Okamura ID: Uveitis II. Peripheral uveitis: Clinical description, complications and differential diagnosis. Am J Ophthalmol 49:1257–66, 1960

Brockhurst RJ, Schepens CL, Okamura ID: Uveitis III. Peripheral uveitis: Pathogenesis, etiology and treatment. Am J Ophthalmol 51:19–26, 1961

Brockhurst RJ, Schepens CL: Uveitis IV: Peripheral uveitis: The complication of retinal detachment. Arch Ophthalmol 80:747–53, 1968

Pruett RC, Brockhurst RJ, Letts N: Fluorescein angiography of peripheral uveitis. Am J Ophthalmol 77:448–53, 1974

Schepens CL: Examination of the ora serrata region: Its clinical significance. In: Acta: 16th Concilium Ophthalmologicum, Britannia, 1950. London, British Medical Association, 1951, vol 2, pp 1384–93

Schepens, CL: L'inflammation de la région de l' "ora serrata" et ses séquelles. Bull Mem Soc Fr Ophtalmol 63:113–25, 1950

Schepens CL: Retinal Detachment and Allied Diseases, vol 2. Philadelphia, Saunders, 1983, pp 672–82

Smith RE, Godfrey SA, Kimura SJ: Chronic cyclitis I. Course and visual prognosis. Trans Am Acad Ophthalmol Otolaryngol 77:760–8, 1973

Smith RE, Godfrey SA, Kimura SJ: Complications of chronic cyclitis. Am J Ophthalmol 82:277–82, 1976

Choroidal Detachments

Bietti GB: Hemorrhagic choroidal detachments. In McPherson A (ed): New and Controversial Aspects of Retinal Detachment. New York, Harper & Row, 1968, pp 471–2

Brav SS: Serous choroidal detachment. Surv Ophthalmol 6:395–415, 1961

Chignell AH: Choroidal detachment following retinal detachment surgery without drainage of subretinal fluid. Am J Ophthalmol 73:860–2, 1972

Gottlieb F: Combined choroidal and retinal detachment. Arch Ophthalmol 88:481–6, 1972

Hawkins WR, Schepens CL: Choroidal detachment and retinal surgery: A clinical and experimental study. Am J Ophthalmol 62:812–19, 1966

Schepens CL: Importance of choroidal detachment in fundus diagnosis. Am J Ophthalmol 51:333–4, 1961

Schepens CL: Retinal Detachment and Allied Diseases, vol 2. Philadelphia, Saunders, 1983, 1003–11

Seelenfreund MH, Kraushar MF, Schepens CL, et al: Choroidal detachment associated with primary retinal detachment. Arch Ophthalmol 91:254–8, 1974

Tolentino FI, Brockhurst RJ: Unilateral scleral icterus due to choroidal hemorrhage. Arch Ophthalmol 70:358–60, 1963

Choroidal Effusion Syndrome

Brockhurst RJ: Nanophthalmos with uveal effusion: A new clinical entity. Trans Am Ophthalmol Soc 72:371–403, 1974

Fogle JA, Green WR: Ciliochoroidal effusion. In Duane TD (ed): Clinical Ophthalmology, vol 4. Philadelphia, Harper & Row, 1981, pp 1–32

McDonald PR, de la Paz Jr V, Sarin LK: Nonrhegmatogenous retinal separation associated with choroidal detachment. Trans Am Ophthalmol Soc 62:226–47, 1964

Schepens CL: Retinal Detachment and Allied Diseases, vol 2.Philadelphia, Saunders, 1983, pp 731–7

Schepens CL, Brockhurst RJ: Uveal effusion. I. Clinical picture. Arch Ophthalmol 70:189–201, 1963

Pigmentary Tumors of the Peripheral Retina

Choroidal Nevi

Ganley LP, Comstock GW: Benign nevi and malignant melanomas of the choroid. Am J Ophthalmol 76:19–25, 1973

Gass JDM: Problems in the differential diagnosis of choroidal nevi and malignant melanomas. The 33rd Edward Jackson Memorial Lecture. Am J Ophthalmol 83:299–323, 1977

Naumann G, Hellner KM, Naumann LR: Pigmented nevi of the choroid. Clinical study of the secondary changes in the overlying tissues. Trans Am Acad Ophthalmol Otolaryngol 75:110–23, 1971

Pro M, Shields JA, Tomer TL: Serous detachment of the forea associated with presumed choroidal nevi. Arch Ophthalmol 96:1374–7, 1978

Shields JA: Tumors of the uveal tract. In

Duane TD (ed): Clinical Ophthalmology, vol 4. Philadelphia, Harper & Row, 1981, pp 1–13

Shields JA, Rodrigues MM, Sarin LK, et al: Lipofuscin pigment over benign and malignant choroidal tumors. Trans Am Acad Ophthalmol Otolaryngol 81:871–81, 1976

Tamler E: A clinical study of choroidal nevi. A follow-up report. Arch Ophthalmol 84:29–32, 1970

Tamler E, Maumanee AE: A clinical study of choroidal nevi. Arch Ophthalmol 62:196–202, 1959

Waltman DD, Gitter KA, Yannuzzi L, et al: Choroidal neovascularization associated with choroidal nevi. Am J Ophthalmol 85:704–10, 1978

Congenital Hypertrophy of the Retinal Pigment Epithelium (CHRPE)

Boldrey EE, Schwartz A: Enlargement of congenital hypertrophy of the pigment epithelium. Am J Ophthalmol 94:64–6, 1982

Buettner H: Congenital hypertrophy of the retinal pigment epithelium. Am J Ophthalmol 79:177–90, 1975

Cleary PE, Gregor Z, Bird AC: Retinal vascular changes in congenital hypertrophy of the retinal pigment epithelium. Br J Ophthalmol 60:499–503, 1976

Kurz GH, Zimmerman LE: Vagaries of the retinal pigment epithelium. Int Ophthalmol Clin 2:441–64, 1962

Norris JL, Cleasby GW: An unusual case of congenital hypertrophy of the retinal pigment epithelium. Arch Ophthalmol 94:1910–11, 1976

Purcell JJ, Shields JA: Hypertrophy with hyperpigmentation of the retinal pigment epithelium. Arch Ophthalmol 93:1122–6, 1975

Reese AB, Jones IS: Benign melanomas of the retinal pigment epithelium. Am J Ophthalmol 42:207–12, 1956

Congenital Grouped Pigmentation (Bear Tracks)

Forsius H, Eriksson A, Nuutlia A, et al: A genetic study of three rare retinal disorders: Dystrophia retinal dysacusis syndrome, X-chromosomal retinoschisis and grouped pigments of the retina. Birth Defects 7:83–98, 1971

Hoeg H: Die gruppierte Pigmentation des Augengrundes. Klin Monatsbl Augenheilkd 49:49–77, 1911

Legrand MJ, Hervouet F, Baron A, et al:

Pigmentation groupée de la rétine. Bull Soc Ophthalmol Fr 64:313–15, 1964

Mauthner L: Lehrbuch der Ophthalmoskopie. Wien, Ed. Fendler, 1868, p 338

Shields JA, Tso MO: Congenital grouped pigmentation of the retina. Arch Ophthalmol 93:1153–5, 1975

Stephenson S: A peculiar form of retinal pigmentation. Trans Ophthalmol Soc UK 11:77, 1891

Waardenberg PJ, Franceschetti A, Klein D: Genetics of and Ophthalmology, vol I. Springfield, IL, Charles C Thomas, 1961, p 548

Metastatic Tumors to the Choroid

Albert DM, Rubenstein RA, Scheie HG: Tumor metastasis to the eye. Part I. Incidence in two-hundred and thirteen adult patients with generalized malignancy. Am J Ophthalmol 63:723–6, 1967

Bloch RS, Gartner S: The incidence of ocular metastatic carcinoma. Arch Ophthalmol 85:673–5, 1971

Davis DL, Robertson DM: Fluorescein angiography of metastatic choroidal tumors. Arch Ophthalmol 89:97–9, 1973

Ferry AP: Lesions mistaken for malignant melanoma of the posterior uvea. Arch Ophthalmol 72:463–9, 1964

Ferry AP: The biological behavior and pathological features of carcinoma metastatic to the eye and orbit. Trans Am Ophthalmol Soc 71:373–425, 1973

Ferry AP, Font RL: Carcinoma metastatic to the eye and orbit. A clinicopathologic study of two-hundred and twenty-seven cases. Arch Ophthalmol 92:276–86, 1974

Fishman M, Tomaszewski M, Kuwabara T: Malignant melanoma of the skin metastatic to the eye. Arch Ophthalmol 9:1309–11, 1976

Gass JDM: Differential Diagnosis of Intraocular Tumors. A Stereoscopic Presentation. St. Louis, Mosby, 1974, pp 140–158

Gitter K, Meyer D, Sarin L, et al: Fluorescein angiography of metastatic choroid tumors. Arch Ophthalmol 89:97–9, 1973

Godtfredsen E: On the frequency of secondary carcinomas in the choroid. Acta Ophthalmol 22:304, 1944

Greear JN: Metastatic carcinoma of the eye. Am J Ophthalmol 33:1015–25, 1950

Greer C: Choroidal carcinoma metastatic from the male breast. Br J Ophthalmol 38:312–15, 1954

Jaeger EA, Frayer WC, Southard ME, et al: Effect of radiation therapy on metastatic choroidal tumors. Trans Am Acad Ophthalmol Otolaryngol 75:94–101, 1971

Reese AB: Tumors of the Eye, 3rd ed. Hagerstown, MD, Harper & Row, 1976, pp 424–31

Shields J: Metastatic tumors to and from the eye. In Croll M, Brady L, Wallner R (eds): Nuclear Ophthalmology. New York, Wiley, 1976, pp 151–60

Usher C: Cases of metastatic carcinoma of the choroid and iris. Br J Ophthalmol 7:10, 1923

Choroidal Melanomas

Callender GR: Malignant melanotic tumors of the eye, a study of histologic types in one hundred and eleven cases. Trans Am Acad Ophthalmol Otolaryngol 36:131, 1931

Callender GR, Wilder HC, Ash JE: Five hundred malignant melanomas of the choroid and ciliary body followed five years or longer. Am J Ophthalmol 25:962–7, 1942

Coleman DJ: Reliability of ocular trauma diagnosis with ultrasound. Trans Am Acad Ophthalmol Otolaryngol 77:677–86, 1973

Davidorf H, Lang JR: The natural history of malignant melanoma of the choroid: Small vs. large tumors. Trans Am Acad Ophthalmol Otolaryngol 79:310–20, 1975

Ferry AP: Lesions mistaken for malignant melanomas of the posterior uvea: A clinicopathologic analysis of one hundred cases with ophthalmoscopically visible lesions. Arch Ophthalmol 72: 463–9, 1964

Font RL, Zimmerman LE, Armaly MF: The nature of the orange pigment over a choroidal melanoma: Histochemical and electron microscopic observations. Arch Ophthalmol 91:359–62, 1974

Gass JDM: Hemorrhage into the vitreous, a presenting manifestation of malignant melanoma of the choroid. Arch Ophthalmol 69:778–9, 1963

Gass JDM: Problems in the differential diagnosis of choroidal nevi and malignant melanomas. The 33rd Jackson Memorial Lecture. Am J Ophthalmol 83:299–323, 1977

Hedges TR, Leopold IH: Parallel retinal folds. Their significance in orbital space taking lesions. Arch Ophthalmol 62:353–5, 1959

Jacobiec FA: Ocular and Adnexal Tumors. Birmingham, AL, Aesculapius, 1978

McLean IW, Foster WD, Zimmerman LE: Prognostic factors in small malignant melanomas of choroid and ciliary body. Arch Ophthalmol 95:48–58, 1977

Newell FW: Choroidal folds. Am J Ophthalmol 75:930–42, 1973

Reese AB: Tumors of the Eye, 3rd ed. Hagerstown, MD, Harper & Row, 1976, pp 193–223

Shields JA: Current approaches to the diagnosis and management of choroidal melanomas. Surv Ophthalmol 21:443–63, 1977

Shields JA, Hagler WS, Federman JL, et al: The significance of the 32-P uptake test in the diagnosis of posterior uveal melanoma. Trans Am Acad Ophthalmol Otolaryngol 79:297–306, 1975

Shields JA, McDonald PR: Improvements in the diagnosis of posterior uveal melanomas. Arch Ophthalmol 91:259–64, 1974

Shields JA, Rodrigues MM, Sarin LK, et al: Lipofuscin pigment over benign and malignant choroidal tumors. Trans Am Acad Ophthalmol Otolaryngol 81:871–81, 1976

Shields JA, Zimmerman LE: Lesions simulating malignant melanoma of the posterior uvea. Arch Ophthalmol 89:466–71, 1973

Zimmerman LE: Problems in the diagnosis of malignant melanomas of the choroid and ciliary body. Am J Ophthalmol 75:917–29, 1970

Zimmerman LE, McLean IW: Changing concepts in the prognosis and management of small malignant melanomas of the choroid. In Peyman CA, Apple DS, Sanders DR (eds): Intraocular Tumors. New York, Appleton-Century-Crofts, 1977, pp 63–74

Retinitis Pigmentosa

Berson FL, Gouras P, Gunkel RD: Rod responses in retinitis pigmentosa dominantly inherited. Arch Ophthalmol 80:58–67, 1968

Berson FL: Light deprivation for early retinitis pigmentosa. Arch Ophthalmol 85:521–9, 1971

Bloome MA, Garcia CA: Rod and cone dystrophies. In Bloome MA, Garcia CA: Manual of Retinal and Choroidal Dystrophies. New York, Appleton-Century-Crofts, 1982, Chapter 5. pp 39–58

Bonavolontar A: La biomicroscopia del vit-

reo nella retinite pigmentosa. Ann Ottal 77:15–20, 1951

Carr RF: Primary retinal degenerations. In Duane TD (ed): Clinical Ophthalmology, vol 3. New York, Harper & Row, 1981, pp 1–19

Deutman AF: Rod-cone dystrophy: Primary, hereditary, pigmentary retinopathy, retinitis pigmentosa. In Archer DB (ed): Krill's Hereditary Retinal and Choroidal Diseases, vol 2: Clinical Characteristics. Hagerstown, MD, Harper & Row, 1977, pp 429–536

Dewar AJ, Reading HW: The biochemical aspects of retinitis pigmentosa. Int J Biochem 6:615–41, 1975

Donders FC: Beiträge zur pathologischen Anatomie des Auges; 2) Pigmentbildung in der Netzhaut. Graefes Arch Ophthalmol 3:139–50, 1857

Francois J: Heredity in Ophthalmology. St. Louis, Mosby, 1961, pp 441–86

Green WR: Retina. In Spencer WH: Ophthalmic Pathology: An Atlas and Textbook, vol. 2, 3rd ed. Philadelphia, Saunders, 1985, pp 1210–21

Liebreich R: Abkunft aus Ehen unter Blutsverwandten als Grund von Retinitis pigmentosa. Dtsch Klin 13:53–5, 1861

Lucas DR: Retinitis pigmentosa. Br J Ophthalmol 40:14–23, 1956

Merin S, Auerbach A: Retinitis pigmentosa. Surv Ophthalmol 20:303–46, 1976

Nishida S, Mizuno K: Electron microscopy of the pigmentary degeneration of the human retina. Acta Soc Ophthalmol Jpn 75:1779–89, 1971

Pillat A: Hintere Glaskörperabhebung bei Retinitis Pigmentosa. Z Augenheilkd. 61:140, 1927

Pruett RC: Retinitis pigmentosa: A biomicroscopical study of irtreous abnormalities. Arch Ophthalmol 93:603–08, 1975

Reiger H: Über die Bedeutung der Aderhautveränderungen für die Entstehung der Glaskörperabhebung. Arch Ophthalmol 136:119–65, 1936

Szamier RB, Berson DL: Retinal ultrastructure in advanced retinitis pigmentosa. Invest Ophthalmol 16:947–62, 1977

Van Trigt AC: De cogspiegel. Thesis. Utrecht, Ned. Lancot (3d ser.) 2:492, 1853

Von Graefe A: Über die Untersuchung des Gesichtsfeldes bei Amblyopischen Affektionen. Graefes Arch Ophthalmol 2:263–4, 282–4, 1856

Developmental Disorders

Colobomas of Retina and Choroid

Coats G: The pathology of coloboma at the nerve entrance. London Ophthalmol Hosp Rep 17:178, 1908

Francois J: Colobomatous malformations of the ocular globe. Int Ophthalmol Clin 8:797–816, 1968

Freeman HM: Congenital retinal diseases. In Tasman WS (ed): Retinal diseases in children. New York, Harper & Row, 1971, pp 4–5

Hird B: An exhaustive treatise on the various colobomas. Ophthalmol Rev 31:162, 1912

Hovland KR, Schepens CL, Freeman HM: Developmental giant retinal tears associated with lens coloboma. Arch Ophthalmol 80:325–31, 1968

Jesberg DO, Schepens CL: Retinal detachment associated with coloboma of the choroid. Arch Ophthalmol 65:163–73, 1961

Pagon RA: Ocular coloboma. Surv Ophthalmol 25:223–6, 1981

Long-Standing Retinal Detachments

Intraocular Fibrosis

Chignell AH: Retinal Detachment Surgery. Berlin, Springer-Verlag, 1980, pp 36–7

Cibis P: Vitreoretinal Pathology and Surgery in Retinal Detachment. St. Louis, Mosby, 1965, pp 77–9

Clarkson JG, Green WR, Massof D: A histopathologic review of 168 cases of preretinal membrane. Am J Ophthalmol 84:1–24, 1977

Constable IF, Oguri M, Chesney CM, et al: Platelet-induced vitreous membrane formation. Invest Ophthalmol 12:680–5, 1973

Constable IJ, Swann DS: Biological vitreous substitutes. Inflammatory response in normal and altered animal eyes. Arch Ophthalmol 88:544–8, 1972

Constable IJ, Tolentino FI, Donovan RH, Schepens CL: Clinico-pathologic correlation of vitreous membranes. In Pruett RC, Regan CDJ (eds): Retina Congress. New York, Appleton-Century-Crofts, 1974, pp 245–57

Foos RY: Anatomic and pathologic aspects of the vitreous body. Trans Am Acad Ophthalmol Otolaryngol 77:171–83, 1973

Gloor BP: Cellular proliferation on the vitreous surface after photocoagulation. Graefes Arch Klin Exp Ophthalmol 178:99–113, 1969

Hogan MJ, Zimmerman LE: Ophthalmic Pathology. Philadelphia, Saunders, 1962, pp 549–68

Jalk AE, Marcos PA, Schepens CL, Azzolini C, Duncan JE, Trempe CL: Surgical treatments of proliferative vitreoretinopathy. Arch Ophthalmol 102: 1135–39, 1984

Lam KW, Ashrafzadeh T, Lee CB: Vitreous membranes. Induction in rabbits by intravitreous leukocyte injections. Arch Ophthalmol 88:655–8, 1972

Laqua H, Machemer R: Glial cell proliferation in retinal detachment (massive periretinal proliferation). Am J Ophthalmol 80:602–18, 1975

Laqua H, Machemer R: Clinico-pathological correlation in massive periretinal proliferation. Am J Ophthalmol 80:913–29, 1975

Leber T: Die Krankheiten der Netzhaut. In Graefe A von, Saemisch ET (eds): Handbuch der Augenheilkunde, vol 3 (2). Leipzig, Englemann, 1915, pp 1501–03

Machemer R: Experimental retinal detachment in the owl monkey. 2. Histology of the retina and pigment epithelium. Am J Ophthalmol 66:396–410, 1968

Machemer R: Pathogenesis and classification of massive periretinal proliferation. Br J Ophthalmol 62:737–47, 1978

Machemer R, Laqua H: Pigment epithelium proliferation in retinal detachment. (Massive periretinal proliferation). Am J Ophthalmol 80:1–23, 1975

Machemer R, Van Horn D, Aaberg TM: Pigment epithelial proliferation in human retinal detachment with massive periretinal proliferation. Am J Ophthalmol 85:181–91, 1978

Magusar MA, Lam KW, Tolentino FL, Liu HS: Lymphocyte-induced vitreous membranes: A comparative study with leukocyte and platelet-induced vitreous membranes. Invest Ophthalmol 14:240–3, 1975

Mandelcorn MS, Machemer R, Fineberg E, Hersch SB: Proliferation and metaplasia of intravitreal retinal pigment epithelium cell autotransplants. Am J Ophthalmol 80:227–37, 1975

Mueller-Jensen K, Machemer R, Azarnia R: Autotransplantation of retinal pigment epithelium in intravitreal diffusion chambers. Am J Ophthalmol 80:530–7, 1975

Parsons JH: The Pathology of the Eye.

Histology. London, Hodder and Stroughton, 1905, pp 542–600

Regnault FR: Vitreous hemorrhage: An experimental study. I. A macroscopic and isotopic study of the evolution of whole blood and hemoglobin. Arch Ophthalmol 83:458–65, 1970

Regnault FR: Vitreous hemorrhage. II. Hemoglobin degradation. Arch Ophthalmol 83:466–9, 1970

Regnault FR: Vitreous hemorrhage. III. Experimental degeneration of the rabbit retina induced by hemoglobin injection into the vitreous. Arch Ophthalmol 83:470–3, 1970

The Retina Society Terminology Committee: The classification of retinal detachment with proliferative vitreoretinopathy. Ophthalmology 90:121–25, 1983

Roth AM, Foos RY: Surface structure of the optic nerve head. I. Epipapillary membranes. Am J Ophthalmol 74:977–85, 1972

Schepens CL: Retinal Detachment and Allied Diseases, vol 2. Philadelphia, Saunders, 1983, pp 177–213.

Smith T: Pathologic findings after retina surgery. In Schepens CL (ed): Importance of the Vitreous Body in Retina Surgery with Special Emphasis on Reoperations. St. Louis, Mosby, 1960, pp 61–93

Teng CC: Discussion of Smith TR: Pathologic findings after retinal surgery. In Schepens CL (ed): Importance of the Vitreous Body in Retina Surgery with Special Emphasis on Reoperations. St. Louis, Mosby, 1960, pp 76–91

Tolentino FI, Schepens CL, Freeman HM: Vitreoretinal Disorders. Diagnosis and Management. Philadelphia, Saunders, 1976, pp 471–89

Van Horn DL, Aaberg TM, Machemer R, Fenzl R: Glial cell proliferation in human retinal detachment with massive periretinal proliferation. Am J Ophthalmol 84:383–93, 1977

Yanoff M, Fine BS: Ocular Pathology. Hagerstown, MD, Harper & Row, 1975, pp 455–562

Zinn K, Constable I, Schepens CL: The fine structure of human vitreous membranes. In Freeman HM, Hirose T, Schepens CL (eds): Vitreous Surgery and Advances in Fundus Diagnosis Treatment. New York, Appleton-Century-Crofts, 1977, pp 34–49

Demarcation Lines

Benson WE, Nantawan P, Morse PH: Characteristics and prognosis of retinal detachments with demarcation lines. Am J Ophthalmol 84:641–4, 1977

Hogan M, Zimmerman LE: Ophthalmic Pathology. Philadelphia, Saunders, 1962, pp 549–68

Schepens CL: Diagnostic and prognostic factors as found in preoperative examination. (Symposium: Retinal Detachment). Trans Am Acad Ophthalmol Otolaryngol 56:398–418, 1952

Retinal Cysts

Chignell AH: Retinal Detachment Surgery. Berlin, Springer-Verlag, 1980, pp 36–7

Hagler WS, North AW: Intraretinal macrocysts and retinal detachment. Trans Am Acad Ophthalmol Otolaryngol 71:442–54, 1967

Ruiz RS: Hemorrhagic macrocyst of the retina. Arch Ophthalmol 83:588–90, 1970

Schepens CL: Retinal Detachment and Allied Diseases, vol 1. Philadelphia, Saunders, 1983, pp 214–32

Schepens CL, Tolentino F, McMeel JW: Diagnostic and prognostic factors as found in preoperative examination. In Pischel D (ed): Retinal Detachment, 2nd ed. Rochester, MN, American Academy of Ophthalmology and Otolaryngology, 1965, pp 51–85

Shrinkage of Retinal Tear Flaps and Opercula

Byer NE: The Peripheral Retina in Profile. A Stereoscopic Atlas. Torrance, CA, Criterion Press, 1982, 159 pp

Rutnin U, Schepens CL: Fundus appearance in normal eyes. IV. Retinal breaks and other findings. Am J Ophthalmol 64:1063–78, 1967

Spencer LM, Straatsma BR, Foos RY: Tractional degenerations of the peripheral retina. In New Orleans Academy of Ophthalmology: Symposium of the Retina and Retinal Surgery. St. Louis, Mosby, 1969, pp 103–27

Index